Collector's Encyclopedia
of
AMERICAN
FURNITURE

Volume 2

Furniture of the Twentieth Century

Robert W. and Harriett Swedberg

COLLECTOR BOOKS
A Division of Schroeder Publishing Co., Inc.

The current values in this book should be used only as a guide. They are not intended to set prices, which vary from one section of the country to another. Auction prices as well as dealer prices vary greatly and are affected by condition as well as demand. Neither the Authors nor the Publisher assumes responsibility for any losses that might be incurred as a result of consulting this guide.

Other Books By Robert W. and Harriett Swedberg

American Clocks and Clockmakers

American Oak Furniture Styles and Prices, revised edition

American Oak Furniture Styles and Prices, Book II, revised edition

American Oak Furniture Styles and Prices, Book III, revised edition

Antiquing in England: A Guide to Antique Centres

Collectors' Encyclopedia of American Furniture, Volume I

Country Furniture and Accessories with Prices

Country Furniture and Accessories with Prices, Book II

Country Pine Furniture Styles and Prices, revised edition

Country Store 'N More

Furniture of the Depression Era

Off Your Rocker

Tins 'N Bins

Victorian Furniture Styles and Prices, revised edition

Victorian Furniture Styles and Prices, Book II

Victorian Furniture Styles and Prices, Book III

Wicker Furniture Styles and Prices, revised edition

ACKNOWLEDGMENTS

Since we do not use photographs from museums in our books, it is necessary to travel extensively in order to obtain appropriate illustrations. We visited many private homes and antique shops in each of these eleven states: Alaska, Illinois, Indiana, Iowa, Kentucky, Michigan, Minnesota, Nebraska, Ohio, Texas and Wisconsin. We are grateful to all of the people who spent many hours with us and helped us move furniture so we could obtain the best possible photographs. We also appreciate the aid of those individuals who did not wish to be acknowledged. Thank you, the named and the unnamed, for providing us with special photographs that will help others who are seeking to learn more about the furniture available during the first fifty or so years of the twentieth century.

ANTIQUE AMERICA
Cheryle, Lance and Norman Frye
Davenport, Iowa

ANTIQUE & SPECIALTY CENTER
Colleen Higgins and Stephen Bunton
Anchorage, Alaska

THE ANTIQUE MALL
Janet Goetz & Grace Jochimsen
Iowa City, Iowa

THE ANTIQUE MARKET
Lincoln, Nebraska

ANTIQUES AT OUR HOUSE
Dick & Bernie King
Minneapolis, Minnesota

BANOWETZ ANTIQUES
Kathy and Virl
Maquoketa, Iowa

BOB'S ANTIQUES
Bob M. DeBerry
Whitewright, Texas

LAURA AND DENNIS BRENNAN

THE BRENNER COLLECTION

BURLINGTON ARCADE
ANTIQUE MALL
Lincoln, Nebraska

ROBERT CARTER

CHITTENDEN & EASTMAN
COMPANY
Burlington, Iowa

LYN AND JAN GALLUP

PHILIP GREGORY
Illinois Antique Center
Peoria, Illinois

GREG'S REFINISHING SHOP
Greg and Dana Whitmer
Manilus, Illinois

BECKY HAWN

ILLINOIS ANTIQUE CENTER
Dan and Kim Philips
Peoria, Illinois

JEFFREY'S ANTIQUE GALLERY
Bryan J. Krick
Findlay, Ohio

J & S ANTIQUES & ANTIQUE MALL
Jim and Sandy Boender
Exit 45 on I-80 near Manilus, Illinois

KIRKHAM'S KORNER ANTIQUES
Dolores and Daniel
Pierceton, Indiana

MONA AND MARC KLARMAN

THE LOUISVILLE ANTIQUE MALL
Harold, Chuck and Don Sego
Louisville, Kentucky

SAM AND LAWANNA McCLURE

MAISON NANETTE
Bed & Breakfast Accomodations and
Antiques
Nanette Wayer
Anchorage, Alaska

OLD EVANSVILLE ANTIQUE MALL
Ed Small
Evansville, Indiana

OLD TYME ANTIQUES
Arcanum, Ohio

BRAD, JAN, RYAN AND SARA PIERCE

REALTY AND AUCTION SERVICE
John A. Whalen
Neapolis, Ohio

RIVER BEND ANTIQUES AND GIFTS
Ronald Bellomy and Laura Heath
Davenport, Iowa

ROCK RIVER ANTIQUE MART
Sally Benson
Rock Island, Illinois

DALE AND VERONICA RUPP

DOUG AND NANCY RUPP

SCHOOL DAYS MALL
Judy and Eric Sewell
Sturtevant, Wisconsin

RANDY SELLBERG

SWEDBERG-REUTER ANTIQUES,
Stripping and Refinishing
Moline, Illinois

DONNA & CHUCK TITUS

TOM'S ANTIQUE CENTER
Centerville, Indiana

BONNIE AND DENTON TUSSING

VICTORIAN BABES ANTIQUES
Vickie Bruss Harter
Arcanum, Ohio

WEBB'S ANTIQUE MALL
Centerville, Indiana

WILLIAMS ANTIQUES
William and Anita Mutch
Anchorage, Alaska

MYRTLE YOLTON

YVONNE MARIE'S
ANTIQUE MALL & COLLECTIBLES
Decatur, Indiana

INTRODUCTION

Furniture from the 1900's through the 1950's is featured in this second volume of the *Collector's Encyclopedia of American Furniture* series. Some examples of oak and its "look-alikes" originated in the late 1800's and they have been included here. Why? Volume 1 emphasized the dark woods (cherry, mahogany, rosewood and walnut) of the nineteenth century. It therefore seemed better to include all of the oak, ash and elm in the second volume of this series even though furniture made from these woods was marketed in the last decade of the nineteenth century.

Classifying furniture by date can always present problems, but we have attempted to put each article included in this book into an age frame according to the following scheme:

Early 1900's	from 1900 to 1915
1920's	from 1916 to 1929
1930's	from 1930 to 1939
1940's	from 1940 to 1949
1950's	from 1950 to 1959

The scores of catalogues we were able to research gave us a great deal of insight into when particular pieces were prevalent, and it was through these references that we were able to become familiar with styles, woods and dates. Included in the text are a series of black and white photographs and some colored ones from early catalogues. These copies show furniture styles that we were not able to photograph due to their inaccessibility.

Then, too, because manufacturers may make the same articles of furniture for a period of consecutive years — in some instances, a score or more — it would be difficult to tell whether the article, a high chair as an example, was made in 1915, when the piece was introduced, or in 1939, when it was still being advertised in furniture catalogues. Due to this factor the dates can only be deemed close approximations.

The prices of furniture and accessories in this book were assigned to them by the dealers and collectors who owned them — a price tag method of assessing values that we have used in all of our books. We, therefore, do not set prices. They are listed as a guide only, and neither the authors nor the publisher assume responsibility for any losses that may be incurred as a result of using this book.

In order to secure photographs for this book, the authors traveled extensively by car. We went south as far as Texas, north to Michigan, east to Ohio, and west to Nebraska. We stopped in adjoining states along the route. We also had the opportunity to fly to Alaska to visit our daughter, Cheryl. While there, we photographed scores of twentieth century furniture items in Anchorage antique shops, where we met native collectors and dealers who invited us into their homes to photograph articles of furniture that would fit into this volume.

Following this introduction are two sections that may prove beneficial to the readers. One is a Patent Number Chart from 1836 through 1959 and the other is a compilation of prices from furniture catalogues covering the first ten years of the twentieth century.

PATENTS

The patent number chart that follows should be helpful in determining the date represented by United States government patent numbers that started in 1836. The single number after each date indicates the beginning number for that year. For the year 1847, for example, the numbering begins at 4,914 and includes all numbers until it reaches 5,408; 5,409 starts the year 1848. This pattern continues through 1959. A chart of this nature has been of invaluable help to us throughout the years in which we have been compiling books on antiques.

The granting of a patent gives its inventor exclusive rights to the manufacture, use and sales of his invention for a period of 17 years. Patent numbers have been found on the backs of iron kitchen cabinet pulls, spring devices found in platform rockers, on labels attached to pieces of furniture, on brass clock works, locks of various kinds and for this volume, we found the patent dates on cedar chests, an accurate way of putting these pieces into a date frame.

YEAR	NUMBER	YEAR	NUMBER	YEAR	NUMBER
1836	1	1878	198,733	1920	1,326,899
1837	110	1879	211,078	1921	1,364,063
1838	516	1880	223,211	1922	1,401,948
1839	1,061	1881	236,137	1923	1,440,362
1840	1,465	1882	251,685	1924	1,478,996
1841	1,923	1883	269,820	1925	1,521,590
1842	2,413	1884	291,016	1926	1,568,040
1843	2,901	1885	310,163	1927	1,612,790
1844	3,395	1886	333,494	1928	1,654,521
1845	3,873	1887	355,291	1929	1,696,897
1846	4,348	1888	375,720	1930	1,742,181
1847	4,914	1889	395,305	1931	1,787,424
1848	5,409	1890	418,665	1932	1,839,190
1849	5,993	1891	443,987	1933	1,892,663
1850	6,981	1892	466,315	1934	1,944,449
1851	7,865	1893	488,976	1935	1,985,878
1852	8,622	1894	511,744	1936	2,026,510
1853	9,512	1895	531,619	1937	2,066,309
1854	10,358	1896	552,502	1938	2,101,004
1855	12,117	1897	574,369	1939	2,142,080
1856	14,009	1898	596,467	1940	2,185,170
1857	16,324	1899	616,871	1941	2,227,418
1858	19,010	1900	640,167	1942	2,268,540
1859	22,477	1901	664,827	1943	2,307,007
1860	26,642	1902	690,385	1944	2,338,081
1861	31,005	1903	717,521	1945	2,366,154
1862	34,045	1904	748,567	1946	2,391,856
1863	37,266	1905	778,834	1947	2,413,675
1864	41,047	1906	808,618	1948	2,433,824
1865	45,685	1907	839,799	1949	2,457,797
1866	51,784	1908	875,679	1950	2,492,944
1867	60,658	1909	908,436	1951	2,536,016
1868	72,959	1910	945,010	1952	2,580,379
1869	85,503	1911	980,178	1953	2,624,016
1870	98,460	1912	1,013,095	1954	2,664,562
1871	110,617	1913	1,049,326	1955	2,698,431
1872	122,304	1914	1,083,267	1956	2,728,913
1873	134,504	1915	1,123,212	1957	2,775,762
1874	146,120	1916	1,166,419	1958	2,813,567
1875	158,350	1917	1,210,389	1959	2,866,973
1876	171,641	1918	1,251,458		
1877	185,813	1919	1,290,027		

PRICES
From Selected Furniture Catalogues, 1901–1910

ARTICLE OF FURNITURE	WOOD OR FINISH	PRICE	
Bed, mantel	Oak	$ 11.00–26.00	
Bed, upright	Oak	$ 25.25–37.25	
	Elm	$ 10.95	
Bed couch	Oak	$ 8.00–29.00	
Bed	Brass	$ 14.90–19.95	
Bed	Iron	$ 2.45–10.45	
Bed lounge	Oak	$ 8.40–15.60	
Bedroom set, 3 pieces	Stained hardwood (golden finish)	$ 15.75–17.25	
	Golden elm	$ 17.50–21.75	
	Golden ash	$ 23.50–25.00	
	Golden oak	$ 19.75–32.50	
	Bird's-eye maple	$ 28.00	
	Mahogany	$ 28.00	
Bookcase desk	Oak	$ 10.75–30.00	
Chair, pressed back (die-cut)	Elm	$ 26.00	dozen
	Oak	$ 43.00	dozen
Chifforobe	Artificially grained oak	$ 15.35–16.95	
Chiffonier	Oak	$ 3.75–10.85	
	Mahogany	$ 13.50	
China buffet with leaded glass	Oak	$ 26.50–33.00	
China cabinet	Quarter sawed oak	$ 8.75–32.25	
Church chair (80" high)	Golden oak	$ 11.70–15.30	
Clock shelf	Oak	$ .40 – 1.50	
Corner cabinet with bent glass	Oak	$ 13.75	
Desk (S-roll), 60" (office desk)	Quarter sawed oak	$ 40.75	
Dresser (Princess)	Oak	$ 9.25–34.75	
Dressing table with French bevel mirror	Oak, mahogany or bird's-eye maple	$ 10.95	
Hall bench with mirror	Oak	$ 13.90–21.50	
Hall tree (oval mirror, lift lid & fancy decoration)	Oak	$ 18.00	
High chair, go cart (Folding Carriage chair)	Oak	$ 6.80	
Hoosier-type cabinet	Oak	$ 20.50–31.00	
Hoosier-type cabinet, made by McDougall (each part is grooved & glued, not nailed)	Oak	$ 42.50–84.00	
Kitchen cabinet	Oak front & elm sides	$ 9.75	
Lady's desk	Oak	$ 5.25 – 9.45	
	Imitation mahogany over birch (Aniline dyed)	$ 9.45	

ARTICLE OF FURNITURE	WOOD OR FINISH	PRICE
Medicine cabinet	Oak or ash	$ 2.40 – 5.50
Mirror, beveled (18" x 40")	Oak	$ 5.50
Morris reclining chair	Golden oak	$ 6.75–16.50
	Quarter sawed oak	$ 8.40–24.60
Music cabinet	Imitation mahogany over birch (Aniline dyed)	$ 5.40 – 9.60
Parlor cabinet	Imitation mahogany over birch (Aniline dyed)	$ 4.85–15.35
Parlor desk	Oak	$ 3.75–12.35
Parlor set, three pieces	Imitation mahogany over birch (Aniline dyed)	$ 19.10–26.10
Parlor table or center table	Oak	$ 1.40 – 5.50
Pier mirror with French bevel	Oak	$ 10.45–19.95
	Curly birch in mahogany finish	$ 10.45–19.95
Plate rack	Selected hardwood	$ .80 – 1.70
Roman chair	Imitation mahogany over birch (Aniline dyed)	$ 3.60 – 5.90
	Quarter sawed oak	$ 4.95 – 9.55
Sideboard	Golden oak	$ 10.75–75.00
Spice cabinet	Selected hardwood	$ .70
Swivel, tilt back office chair (called Spring and Screw)	Elm	$ 4.60 – 4.95
	Quarter sawed oak	$ 5.35 – 8.65
Table, claw foot extension, 45" top	Oak	$ 11.85–17.25
Table, claw foot extension, 52" top	Oak	$ 28.25
Table, rectangular extension	Oak	$ 6.65–18.45
Umbrella rack	Oak	$ 1.70 – 2.50
Wall pocket	Selected hardwood	$ .50 – 1.50
Wardrobe	Oak	$ 6.60–15.00
Washstand	Elm	$ 4.50
	Ash	$ 5.25
	Oak	$ 5.75

Encyclopedia Listings
of
AMERICAN FURNITURE

ANILINE DYE

Synthetic dye produced from coal-tar products is called aniline dye. It can be purchased in powder form in a wide range of colors, and originally was dissolved in oil or mineral spirits. It bled into varnish so a protective coating of shellac had to be applied over the stain. Later water or denatured alcohol was used as a solvent. Alcohol was better because it did not raise the grain of the wood. After the first application dried, more dye was frequently applied to obtain a deeper hue and since bleeding was no longer a problem, varnish could be brushed directly over the surface when it dried.

Aniline dye, applied to birch and to some varieties of beech and maple, was an attempt to imitate the colors of cherry and mahogany at a time when these hardwoods were becoming scarce. Its use began in the late 1800's. In 1902, a furniture catalogue pictured birch chairs finished mahogany and also showed dainty divans, perhaps big enough to seat two. The distributor featured three-piece "birch finished mahogany parlor sets" that cost $19.10 to $26.10. Some had inlaid mother-of-pearl designs on the back frames.

Attempts to strip the finish from pieces of furniture treated with aniline dye are futile because this stain penetrates so deeply that red streaks will remain after the stripping process.

Mahogany stained (aniline dyed) rocker with mahogany veneered splat, shell decoration on back rail and upholstered seat, early 1900's. 24" arm to arm, 42" high.

ART DECO

This name developed after the Paris Exposition in 1966 that commemorated the earlier "Exposition Internationale des Arts Décoratifs et Industriels Modernes" held in France in 1925. This style was originally called Art Moderne or Art Décoratif. Art Deco was a shortened version of the latter. Its influence in furniture styles peaked in the United States between 1925 and 1935. Currently the popularity of Art Moderne is experiencing a rebirth.

Designers were eclectic, borrowing from many sources. Furniture in step shapes was influenced by Aztec temples. From Africa came the idea for blackamoors, figures of dark-skinned people, which were used at times as arm supports on chairs or for pedestals on tables. Black lacquer represents an Oriental influence. Carvings on furniture included feathers, tassels, sunbursts, drapes, baskets of fruits, and garlands. Bright greens, silver, reds, gold, purple, and especially orange were popular colors.

Upholstery featured lush fabrics including mohair and furs, fake leather and real or man-made leopard skin. On occasion onyx, a variety of agate, was used for table tops. Metal bedroom sets were often painted or could be disguised with a false walnut grain. Chromium or chrome, a hard metallic chemical element that resists corrosion, was used to plate ashtrays, chairs, and table legs. Some wooden tables and chairs featured ribbed legs. Composition tops were made frequently. Handles were often formed

Mahogany stained (aniline dyed) maple arm chair with bird's-eye maple splat, claw feet and upholstered seat, early 1900's. 24" arm to arm, 35" high.

from Bakelite, the first synthetic resin. It was created by and named for the Belgium-born United States chemist Leo Hendrick Baekeland who developed this plastic in 1909. The aforementioned characteristics demonstrate the dramatic qualities of Art Moderne or Art Deco styles.

Oriental style chest of drawers with black lacquer finish, gold trim, raised design on top drawer and leather inset on the top, late 1930's. 29" wide, 16" deep, 30" high.

Walnut and V-matched Orientalwood veneer double closet chifforobe, manufactured by Globe Bosse World Furniture Company, 1930's. 39" wide, 21" deep, 69" high.

Four-piece mahogany veneered bedroom suite with painted cream lines, 1920's. Bed — 56" wide, 41" high headboard, 23" high footboard. Vanity — 42" wide, 18" deep, 65" high. Bench — 23" wide, 13" deep, 19" high. Chest of drawers — 32" wide, 18" deep, 49" high.

Mahogany and crotch mahogany veneered liquor cabinet with center drop lid flanked by convex glass doors on top and veneered doors below. Inner light turns on when drop lid is opened. Trademarked "Beautility." Early 1930's. 54" wide, 20" deep, 35" high.

ART NOUVEAU

Europe experienced a revival of interest in the decorative arts in the late 1800's. This "New Art" frequently adopted Japanese motifs. Nature inspired artists. The butterfly, deep-sea creatures, swans and peacocks appeared. The languid curves of flower stalks held buds or pale blossoms. The tall and sensuous figures of young girls appeared to be wavy or floating. Dim and shadowy effects yielded a dreamy quality to artistic creations. Straight lines were out and curves were in demand. Typical lines were long, slightly curved, and could terminate suddenly in a whiplash sharp curve.

Art Nouveau was short lived. After the first decade of the 1900's, its popularity began to wane. It faded out around the 1920's. The beauty of his lamps, vases and leaded glass windows won Louis Comfort Tiffany the title of the leading exponent of the Art Nouveau style in the United States. Not a great deal of American furniture was produced in the Art Nouveau style. Fine examples of Art Nouveau furniture, mainly by French designers, can be found in *The Complete Book of Collecting Art Nouveau* by John Mebane, 1970, published by Weathervane Books, New York.

ARTIFICIAL GRAINING

When paint or stain is applied to furniture to imitate the grain or figure of a specific wood, it is called artificial graining. The pattern can be put on with special combs, patterned rollers, sponges, stamps, feathers or by other means. Much graining was done during the nineteenth century on pine and light wood pieces. In the twentieth century, the 1927 Sears, Roebuck Catalogue advertised dining room sets "solidly constructed of hardwood in imitation quarter-sawed oak." Furniture with imitation graining, less expensive to produce than objects made from genuine oak, provided the customer with a look-alike oak at an affordable price.

Artificially oak grained commode washstand, 1920's. 30" wide, 17" deep, 29" high, 4" back rail.

BAKER'S CABINET

This is a current term for a cupboard that evolved from a table with features such as a flour bin, pull-out boards for kneading dough and for cutting, perhaps a divided bin with sugar in one section and meal in the other and drawers for cutlery and linens. Later, when enclosed shelves were added on top of the table, the cabinet was complete. A housewife had one unit in which she could store her essential cooking needs and have a work space as well. These features were advertised as labor saving conveniences.

BARBER'S CABINET

This was a place where a barber kept his supplies. When a shop had many workers, space was provided in a long, mirrored back bar for each barber's equipment. A chair sat in front of each section. Both the small and large versions are, at times, incorporated into home decors.

BED

In the 1800's the word *bed* referred to some type of covering stuffed with a filling such as straw or feathers. The bedstead was the structure which supported it. Now the term *bed* is used to signify the frame that holds a mattress. Many of the wooden bedsteads of the 1800's were tall and oversized with applied or carved decorations. The most common wood of the Victorian age (circa 1840–1900) was solid walnut. Just prior to the arrival of the new century, more variety appeared and look-alike ash and oak became prominent.

Listed in the Chittenden & Eastman Co. (Burlington, Iowa) catalogue No. 81, dated May 1, 1899, are bedsteads made of hardwood, oak, ash, and maple. Designs, now referred to as applied because they are made separately and attached to the piece, were used. Also, scooped out carving, currently called "spoon carving," provided decoration.

Wooden folding beds were also in evidence in this catalogue. One version was a mantel bed of oak or ash with a French beveled mirror above a shelf. It measured 4' x 6' inside. It stood upright when not serving as a sleeping site and resembled a mantel. The tendency is to call such a unit by the generic name "Murphy Bed." Examples of these upright folding beds are seldom found today. For more information, see "Murphy Bed."

Iron beds were depicted in this same catalogue. Some featured brass tips, termed *vases*; on others brass scrolls appeared on head and foot boards. Beds made entirely of brass were available, too. Metal beds in a 1905–06 catalogue featured a finish called "Vernis Martin," described as the best solid gold bronze finish. It would not tarnish or rub off. Green, white or blue could be obtained also. This varnish process, originally introduced by the Martin Brothers during the reign of France's Louis XIV, 1638–1715,

Oak, pine and cherry baker's cabinet, early 1900's. 42" wide, 29" deep, 70" high.

Pair of oak barber's cabinets with attached mirrors, early 1900's. 22" wide, 14" deep, 66" high.

emulated Oriental lacquering. It was applied to achieve brilliance and depth in furniture finishes.

In a 1952–53 catalogue, various steel beds were featured. A molded tubing version was available with a brown enamel or grained walnut finish. Some showed stencil panels in the middle of head and foot boards. Others had waterfall tops, straight posts and a two-toned grained walnut or a blond finish.

Single or double beds were common during the first fifty years of the twentieth century. A new phrase, *twin beds*, identified two matching singles. In the 1950's, some bunk beds could be used as singles or could be stacked one above the other. Often a ladder was included to reach the top bunk. Some of the units were of solid maple. Others were of inexpensive gumwood with a maple stain.

A study of old furniture catalogues reveals the evolution and diversification of bed styles. By 1912 a genuine mahogany poster bed, priced at $90.00, was on the market. The posts were six feet high. In 1920 a bow end bed with low head and foot boards was stylish.

Oak bed with applied decorations, early 1900's. 56" wide, 55" high headboard, 33" high footboard.

Oak bed with applied decorations and carved head near top of headboard, early 1900's. Manufactured by Aulsbrook & Sturges, Sturgis, Michigan. 57" wide, 79" high headboard. Matching dresser was not photographed.

Oak bed with applied decorations, early 1900's. 58" wide, 77" high headboard, 39" high footboard.

Mahogany veneered four poster bed with incised lines and applied decorations, late 1920's to early 1930's. 56" wide, 50" high headboard, 49" high footboard.

Brass and black painted metal bed, early 1900's. 62" wide, 66" high headboard, 48" high footboard.

Ash bed with incised decorations, late 1800's to early 1900's. 41" wide, 60" high headboard, 31" high footboard.

BEDROOM SUITE OR SET

A simple bedroom set consisted of a bed, a chest of drawers, and a dresser. A larger suite had a greater number of pieces, possibly including a rocker, chair, dressing table and stool, bedside tables, and assorted clothes chests.

As the 1890's closed, ash and oak had become the prominent furniture woods. By 1910 different woods were introduced, including a walnut finish over selected hardwoods, circassian walnut, mahogany finish on birch, genuine mahogany veneer, quarter sawed red gum, bird's-eye maple, solid mahogany, genuine black walnut, an ivory enamel finish and an imitation quarter sawed oak finish.

Sets from the middle teens through the 1920's copied previous classical styles encompassing designs from the sixteenth century Italian Renaissance, Late Stuart (1688), seventeenth century Jacobean, the Adam Period, William and Mary, Queen Anne with flowing contours, Late Georgian with simple and dignified lines, Hepplewhite with tapered legs that had a slight outward splay, and Louis XVI, a style that revolted against the ornate, rococo furniture.

Waterfall sets, using a variety of imported veneers, were introduced in the late 1930's. Woods included American sliced walnut with genuine marquetry trim inlay on drawers, and zebrawood decorations on avodire and gum. Instead of straight edges on chests of drawers, dressers, vanities and bed head and foot boards, a rounded edge was present. This gave the sets their descriptive title *waterfall*. A large round mirror often without a frame was included on vanities. A drop center vanity, available in the 1940's, had a middle section that was lower than its flanking drawers or doors. The last waterfall bedroom set noted appeared in a 1959 catalogue advertisement.

15

Catalogue accounts from the early 1950's mentioned square lines and a blond satinwood finish over Southern hardwood. Limed oak over Western larchwood also had a square configuration. Woods of this period included magnolia, gum, hackberry, larchwood, walnut and oak veneer, avodire and Philippine mahogany. Limed oak and maple furniture abounded. Unfinished furniture that one could stain was a do-it-yourself challenge.

Ash two-piece bedroom set, early 1900's. Left: Commode washstand with serpentine front — 31" wide, 19" deep, 26" high. Right: Dresser with serpentine front, applied decorations and swing mirror — 41" wide, 20" deep, 73" high.

Four-piece bird's-eye maple and maple bedroom set, 1920's. Left: Vanity with three mirrors and decks — 38" wide, 20" deep, 61" high. Bench — 23" wide, 14" deep, 19" high. Center: Dresser with swing mirror — 46" wide, 22" deep, 76" high. Right: Four poster bed — 56" wide, 62" high.

Oak three-piece bedroom set, early 1900's. Top: Bed with applied decorations — 56" wide, 84" high headboard, 37" high footboard. Left: Dresser with serpentine front, applied decorations and swing mirror — 44" wide, 21" deep, 76" high. Right: Commode washstand with serpentine projection top drawer and applied decorations on attached towel rack — 34" wide, 18" deep, 44" high.

Curly maple three-piece bedroom set, early 1900's. Top: Bed with applied decorations — 57" wide, 79" high headboard. Dresser with serpentine front and applied decorations on swing mirror frame — 49" wide, 23" deep, 82" high. Commode washstand with serpentine front and applied decorations on attached towel bar rack — 38" wide, 18" deep, 58" high.

Oak three-piece bedroom set (bed not pictured), early 1900's. Left: Dresser with applied decorations on mirror frame — 45" wide, 20" deep, 79" high. Right: Commode washstand with attached towel bar rack — 32" wide, 18" deep, 55" high.

Four-piece bedroom set with walnut burl veneers on drawer fronts, oak sides, oak veneer tops and oak applied decorations on drawer fronts, 1930's. (Bed not pictured.) Label on back reads "J.H. Wiley, The Furniture Man, 280–98 Market St., San Francisco." Left: Dresser — 48" wide, 20" deep, 72" high. Middle: Chest of drawers — 36" wide, 18" deep, 48" high. Right: Night stand — 16" wide, 15" deep, 27" high.

Six-piece burl veneered bedroom set, 1930's, with applied decorations, serpentine sides on case pieces, zebrawood veneer banding around drawers, edges of tops and around bed panels. Multicolored dyed marquetry fruit basket design on case fronts and mottled avodire veneer on long drawers of case pieces. Metal plaque reads "Herman Miller Furniture Co., Zeeland, Michigan, *The All-Walnut Line*." Top, left: Bed — 57" wide, 46" high headboard, 25" high footboard. Top, right: Chest of drawers — 46" wide, 20" deep, 42" high. Middle, left: Dresser — 56" wide, 25" deep, 33" high. Middle, right: Vanity — 52" wide, 20" deep, 32" high. Below, left: Vanity bench — 30" wide, 15" deep, 22" high. Below, right: Night stand — 15" wide, 14" deep, 29" high.

Four-piece waterfall bedroom set with mahogany, walnut and zebrawood veneers and selected hardwood stiles and trim, late 1930's or early 1940's. Top: Bed — 56" wide, 41" high headboard, 25" high footboard. Left: Dressing table with attached mirror — 44" wide, 16" deep, 65" high. Bench — 23" wide, 14" deep, 18" high. Right: Chest of drawers — 30" wide, 16" deep, 48" high.

Four-piece waterfall bedroom set with bleached mahogany veneers, late 1930's or early 1940's. Top: Bed — 56" wide, 52" high headboard, 40" high footboard. Left: Dressing table — 42" wide, 17" deep, 62" high. Bench — 14" wide, 22" deep, 18" high. Right: Chest of drawers — 30" wide, 16" deep, 47" high.

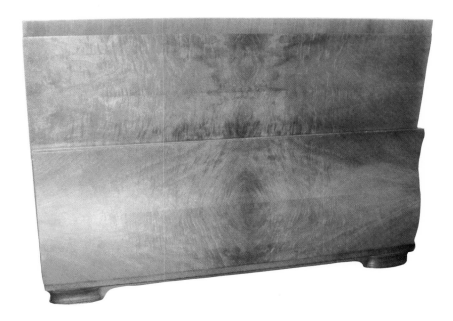

Four-piece mahogany veneered bedroom set, late 1930's to late 1940's. Top: Bed with matched veneer panels — 56" wide, 40" high headboard, 24" high footboard. Left: Vanity with round mirror, swell side drawer fronts and concave central drawer — 50" wide, 19" deep, 65" high. (Bench not pictured.) Right: Chest of drawers with serpentine drawer fronts and matched veneer panels — 36" wide, 20" deep, 52" high.

Three-piece bedroom set with applied decorations, V-matched mahogany veneer panels, and zebrawood and oak veneer on fronts, 1920's. Left: Chifforette with cedar lined right hand side compartment — 37" wide, 19" deep, 66" high. Right: Four poster bed — 56" wide, 56" high headboard, 49" high footboard. (Dresser not pictured.)

Four-piece native American cherry bedroom set with Terratone finish as pictured and priced in 1954 – 55 *Square Brand Catalogue*. Bed — 54" wide. Double dresser — 54" wide, 20" deep, 61" high. Chest of drawers — 39" wide, 20" deep, 48" high.

BENCH

A bench, with or without a back, is a long seat that can accommodate several people. It served in many places. Near a radio was a bench on which the listener sat to turn the dials. Others accompanied vanity or dressing tables. Benches were used in breakfast areas to seat family members. Rustic wash types upon which tubs sat on Monday wash day, farm benches, pews from churches, railroad benches, those with advertising on them, and other versions are now retrieved to become a part of home decors.

Oak bench with perforated design on the back, found in shoe department of hardware store, 1920's. Similar benches were used in railroad depots. 60" wide, 18" deep, 36" high.

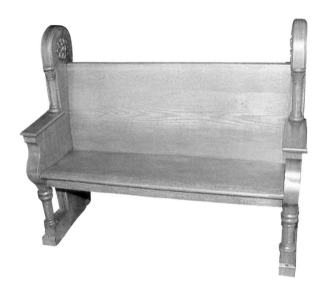

Oak church bench with carved flower design on each end, 1920's. 45" wide, 19" deep, 41" high.

Oak bench with arms and splatted back, early 1900's. 50" arm to arm, 20" deep, 37" high.

Oak church bench, 1920's. 50" wide, 21" deep, 36" high.

Oak Roman bench with upholstered seat and splayed legs, early 1900's. 20" wide, 14" deep, 18" high.

BENTWOOD FURNITURE

Around 1840 Michael Thonet of Vienna, Austria constructed light, strong, inexpensive chairs by bending steamed wood rods in a manner that scientifically used the strength of the individual parts. Tables and other types of furniture were made by this new method. Ice cream chairs of the early 1900's were often of bentwood, as were lodge chairs. Bentwood continues to be produced and a favorite is the rocker with its continuously rounded lines.

Bird's-eye maple chiffonier with serpentine front and attached swing mirror, 1920's. 34" wide, 19" deep, 70" high.

Maple bentwood swing cradle on frame, 1940's. 41" long, 22" deep, 40" high.

BIRD'S – EYE MAPLE

A bird's-eye pattern is produced by cutting at a tangent through the indentations that sometimes appear in the annual rings of trees. They are found more commonly in maple than in other species of trees. Generally it is used as a veneer because it goes further that way. It can be sliced 1/28" thick and can be applied over a base wood that gives it strength. This enables the figural pattern from one tree to cover many pieces of furniture. Bedroom sets, tables and occasional chairs of the 1920's were produced with bird's-eye maple veneered surfaces.

BLEACHED OR BLOND FINISH

A bleached or blond finish is achieved by using a strong bleach to tone down the color of the wood, after which a clear varnish is applied. This process works well on light colored, close grained hardwoods like oak. Sometimes a pale colored paint is wiped on and then off the sanded surface of the wood to achieve a blond finish. These techniques were in vogue in the 1950's.

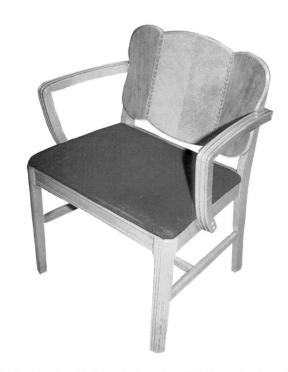

Vanity bench with bleached and artificially grained mahogany back and birch base, 1940's. Manufactured by Broyhill Furniture Factories, Lenoir Furniture Corporation; Lenoir, North Carolina. 24" wide, 31" high.

Left: Bleached oak chest of drawers, sold by Lammerts of St. Louis, 1950's. Part of a five-piece bedroom set. 36" wide, 19" deep, 43" high.

Governor Winthrop style fall front secretary with block front, 1927. 30" wide, 15" deep, 78" high.

BLOCKFRONT

Blockfronts originated as an American design executed on desks, cabinets, chests or other case pieces in the 1760's to 1780's and are usually associated with craftsmen in the Newport, Rhode Island area. Some, however, were made in Massachusetts and Connecticut as well. The name was fitting because the fronts of these pieces were broken vertically into three distinct raised panels or blocks. Two men, John Goddard and his son-in-law, John Townsend, are closely associated with this style's development. Manufacturers in the late 1920's revived the blockfront look. The painted surface secretary with a broken pediment (a decorative top piece that does not meet completely at the center) and block front drawers that is illustrated here was purchased in 1927. Examples were made in the 1930's as well because furniture manufacturers sought to emulate quality furniture designs from the past.

BOOKCASE

Many varieties of cabinets to house books are available. While some are simply racks or open rows of shelves, other forms include both a desk and bookcase — commonly called a bookcase-desk combination. This type was extremely popular during the first several decades of the twentieth century and most were of oak. These desks, when found in early 1900's catalogues, were simply called bookcases. Currently they are referred to as secretaries or side-by-sides.

Other examples included the single, double and triple glass door bookcases, the stack variety which was purchased in individual units, and the secretary type with a desk base and glass enclosed bookcase top.

Oak single door bookcase with applied winged decoration on back rail, 1920's. 29" wide, 10" deep, 50" high.

Left: Oak single door bookcase with grotesques on stiles, rolled apron base and claw feet, early 1900's. 30" wide, 17" deep, 59" high, 5" back rail. Middle: Oak single door bookcase, early 1900's. 27" wide, 12" deep, 62" high. Right: Oak folding bookcase with hinged sides, 1920's. 30" wide, 11" deep, 48" high, 8" gallery.

Above: Mahogany stained double door bookcase, early 1900's. 43" wide, 12" deep, 54" high. Right: Oak double door bookcase made in a high school wood shop, dated 1925. 48" wide, 13" deep, 66" high.

Oak three-door bookcase with two drawers in center section, incised lines and applied decorations, late 1800's or early 1900's. 60" wide, 13" deep, 69" high, 13" back rail.

Oak bookcase with convex glass door and swell drawer, two flat glass doors, lion's heads and grotesques on back rail and mirror frame and claw feet, early 1900's. 51" wide, 13" deep, 72" high.

Oak bookcase with leaded and stained glass, incised carving and claw feet, early 1900's. 48" wide, 13" deep, 65" high.

BOOKCASE DESK COMBINATION

A bookcase desk combination was more often made to accommodate right-handed people than those who are left-handed. For the former, the desk is on the right so the user can reach for a book with the left hand. Conversely, the desk is on the left for the convenience of a left-handed person. Some more expensive, ambidextrous versions feature a bookcase on each side of the fall front writing surface.

Mahogany bookcase desk combination with convex glass and swell top drawer, early 1900's. 39" wide, 13" deep, 73" high.

Right, top: Oak bookcase desk combination with convex glass, projection swell drawer, incised lines, applied decorations and claw feet, early 1900's. 38" wide, 14" deep, 69" high.

Right, bottom: Oak bookcase desk combination with convex glass, incised lines and applied decorations, early 1900's. 37" wide, 13" deep, 69" high.

Oak bookcase desk combination with convex glass, ogee top drawer, incised lines, claw feet and two mirrors, one flanked by carved grotesques, late 1800's or early 1900's. 42" wide, 16" deep, 74" high.

Oak bookcase desk combination with projection drawer and applied decorations, early 1900's. Plaque on back reads, "Presented to the Rev. S. & Mrs. Langdon on completion of three years faithful service in the Aldershot & Farnham Circuit. By their many friends as a slight token of esteem & affection. August 1903." 41" wide, 14" deep, 74" high.

Oak bookcase desk combination with convex glass, swell drawer, applied decorations and a grotesque in the center of the hood on the bookcase back, early 1900's. 42" wide, 15" deep, 73" high.

Oak bookcase desk combination with applied decorations on drop front and back rail, early 1900's. 39" wide, 13" deep, 66" high.

Oak Mission style bookcase desk combination, early 1900's. 36"
wide, 13" deep, 63" high.

Oak bookcase desk combination with applied decorations and
scroll feet, called colonial style in early catalogues, 1920's. 37"
wide, 12" deep, 71" high.

Oak bookcase desk combination with convex glass, leaded glass
door, bonnet hood, applied decorations and claw feet, 1920's.
42" wide, 17" deep, 78" high.

BORAX

"Borax" was the name applied to the lower priced,
mass produced, poorly made, showy furniture of the 1920's
and 1930's. It was often stained walnut or mahogany or
artificially grained over a base wood such as gum wood.
Instead of using real veneer, manufacturers used veneerite.
These were strips of veneer patterns printed on paper and
applied to the furniture to imitate an inlay design of different
colored woods. These strips peel off, causing the pattern to
disappear, when paint remover is applied to the surface.
Three-ply instead of five-ply tops and sides were present on
this furniture. Borax pieces can be restored by staining,
artificially graining, antiquing, painting or leaving them in
their natural wood color, protected by several coats of
varnish, after the original finish has been taken off with
paint remover.

Three-piece bedroom set, called borax style, with router lines and artificially grained surfaces over selected hardwoods, 1920's. Bed — 57" wide, 49" high headboard, 23" high footboard. Dressing table — 42" wide, 17" deep, 66" high. Chest of drawers — 32" wide, 17" deep, 44" high, 4" back rail.

BREAKFAST SET (see Dinette Set)

Dining sets comprising four chairs and a table, or two benches and a table, were labeled breakfast or dinette sets and were prominent in 1920–1930 catalogues. Some examples continued to be shown in later catalogues. They were extremely popular because of their space-saving size. Many tables had drop leaves. Made of selected hardwoods, including elm, oak and ash, these sets were generally painted in a wide range of colors. The two-toned choices of frosted silver gray oak or frosted golden brown with router-line divisions were offered in a 1927 furniture catalogue. One table had a reproduction burl walnut top with all other parts finished in a choice of Chinese red or sage green. The back rails, the feet of the chairs, and the edges and feet of the table were finished in black. On many sets pretty floral transfer patterns in bright colors appeared on the backs of chairs, table legs and table tops.

Left: Oak five-piece breakfast set comprising four chairs, one of which is pictured with the table, 1940's. Chairs decorated with red butterflies and yellow flowers with green stems on top slats and seat fronts, 34" high. Table is decorated in the same manner at each corner of the top, 42" x 30", 30" high, one 12" leaf. Right: Another view of the oak five-piece breakfast set, showing the table and two chairs, after it was refinished naturally.

Five-piece breakfast set with four painted chairs, 1950's. Chairs — 35" high. Porcelain top table with white painted wooden base — 40" x 25", 31" high, 10" leaf extension on each side of table.

Oak side chair, 35" high, 1930's, from a five-piece breakfast set including table, one arm chair and three side chairs.

Waterfall buffet with V-matched quarter-sawed Orientalwood and zebrano veneers, late 1930's or early 1940's. Part of a nine-piece dining set. 59" wide, 19" deep, 38" high, 9" mirror back.

BUREAU COMMODE

A small chest of drawers upon which a bowl and pitcher was placed, in pre-plumbing days, was called a bureau commode. Towels, wash cloths, soap, and other personal grooming aids could be kept in the drawers. This type of commode, more characteristic of the nineteenth century, was replaced as the new century dawned by washstand commodes. The washstand commode has a combination of doors and drawers, a towel bar top, and often an attached mirror.

BUFFET (see Sideboard)

A buffet or sideboard is a dining room piece with drawers and cupboard where silverware, china, linens and other mealtime items can be stored.

Oak Mission style china buffet, early 1900's. 55" wide, 18" deep, 41" high, 10" mirror back.

Elm and ash bureau commode with applied decorations on splash back, early 1900's. 31" wide, 16" deep, 29" high, 7" splash back.

CABINET (see China Cabinet and Hoosier Cabinet)

Storage cabinets, such as music, medicine, Hoosier and china, were available for holding records and sheet music, first aid and shaving supplies, kitchen wares and baking needs, and glass and china items. The purpose of each determined its name.

Painted and stencil designed cabinet, 1930's. Currently used as a jewelry stand. 11" wide, 8" deep, 48" high.

Oak medicine cabinet, 1920's. 17" wide, 8" deep, 29" high.

CANE CHAIR

A chair that is caned has a woven rattan seat. It can be hand done when there are holes surrounding the perimeter of the seat through which the rattan is laced. When a groove surrounds the seat, a wet pre-woven sheet of cane is cut to fit and a spline strip is forced into and glued in the groove to keep the cane snugly in place. Some chairs and rockers may have cane backs.

Oak cane seat chair, early 1900's. Part of a dining room set with six chairs and a table. 39" high.

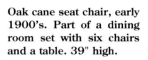

Oak music cabinet, 1920's. 19" wide, 12" deep, 30" high, 13" mirror back.

CAPTAIN'S CHAIR

This name is applied to a debased Windsor-type chair with spindles, a wooden seat and a continuous back and arms. An American Windsor from the late 1700's and early 1800's was skillfully crafted by hand with splayed, canted or slanted out legs extending up through its shaped, solid seat. The debased captain's chair was popular in offices, saloons, club rooms, fire stations, and aboard river boats. They were produced generously and are still manufactured today.

Oak captain's chair with hand hold in back rail, early 1900's. 22" arm to arm, 31" high.

Pine and maple captain's chair, 1920's. 22" arm to arm, 28" high.

CEDAR CHEST

The introduction of the cedar chest in the 1920's provided the homemaker with a cedar or cedar-lined, lift lid chest that stored and protected garments, blankets and furs from moth damage. The first examples were constructed of cedar and frequently had wide copper bands on the outside. As time passed the exposed cedar was covered with various species of decorative veneers. The 1930's saw the emergence of the waterfall style with its rolled top that continued in use into the 1950's. As that decade closed this style faded away and once again square lines appeared.

Walnut veneered and selected hardwoods cedar chest with applied decoration and ring molding on front, 1920's. 40" wide, 17" deep, 19" high.

Walnut veneered Cavalier cedar chest with incised lines, applied decorations and bird's-eye maple veneer panel on front, late 1920's. Made by Tennessee Furniture Corporation, Chattanooga. 44" wide, 19" deep, 25" high.

Walnut and Orientalwood V-matched veneered waterfall cedar chest, 1940's. 45" wide, 19" deep, 25" high.

CELLARETTE

Because cellar can refer to a room were wines are kept, manufacturers coined the word *cellarette* for a small liquor cabinet that was described in 1905 – 1906 and 1906 – 1907 furniture catalogues. No other catalogues from the late 1800's through the 1950's that were inspected listed them. From 1920 through 1933, liquor cabinets were not manufactured because of the Prohibition Amendment to the United States Constitution which prohibited the brewing and selling of alcoholic beverages.

Oak combination liquor and smoking cabinet that has space for poker chips and cards, early 1900's. Claw feet and incised design on front door. View on the right shows the interior of the cabinet. 22" wide, 17" deep, 38" high, 4" rail.

Matched mahogany veneered cellarette, early 1900's. View on the right shows the interior of the cabinet. 24" wide, 13" deep, 39" high.

CHAIR

Chairs often received their names from their shapes, uses, construction characteristics and styles. Barrel, arm, and wing fit into the shape category while dining and office chairs indicate a special use. In the construction area, overstuffed, easy and reclining Morris chairs provide comfort. Saddle seat, cobbler seat, cane seat, pressed back and bentwood also fit into this classification. The straight line Mission and the curvaceous Queen Anne with its cabriole legs are examples of period styles.

Elm and maple pressed back, wooden seat chair, early 1900's. One of a set of six. 39" high.

Oak, elm and maple pressed back, wooden seat chair, early 1900's. One of a set of eight. 37" high.

Oak double pressed back, cane seat chair, early 1900's. One of a set of six. 38" high.

Left: Elm pressed back, cane seat chair, early 1900's. 40" high.

Right: Oak cane seat chair with finger hold on back rail, 1920's. 33" high.

Oak pressed back, cane seat chair with incised decoration, late 1800's or early 1900's. One of a set of six. 40" high.

Oak double pressed back, cane seat chair, early 1900's. One of a set of four. 41" high.

Oak triple pressed back, cane seat chair, early 1900's. One of a set of eight. 39" high.

Oak side chair with imitation leather seat, applied decorations and hand hold on back panel, early 1900's. One of a set of six. 38" high.

Oak chair with pressed cane seat and back, early 1900's. 37" high.

Birch cane seat chair with bleached mahogany veneered back and applied decoration, early 1900's. 38" high.

Mahogany stained birch (aniline dyed) side chair with painted decorations on back rails, seat and legs, late 1800's or early 1900's. 39" high.

Oak fancy back side chair with upholstered seat and back panel, early 1900's. 45" high.

Oak arm chair with carved decorations and grotesques on back rail and slat, early 1900's. 22" arm to arm, 40" high.

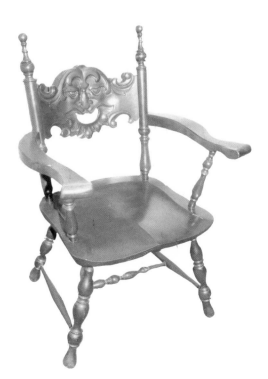

Left: Mahogany stained birch (aniline dyed) arm chair with Man of the Wind on back rail, late 1800's or early 1900's. 26" arm to arm, 41" high.

Right: Mahogany stained birch (aniline dyed) arm chair with carved grotesque on back rail, saddle seat and cabriole legs, early 1900's. 24" arm to arm, 34" high.

Oak arm chair with scooped oak veneered seat and incised decorations on back panel, early 1900's. 25" arm to arm, 40" high.

CHEVAL DRESSER

A tall swinging mirror mounted on a frame is a cheval mirror. When the mirror, along with a hat box, sits atop a low chest of drawers, the resulting bedroom piece is called a cheval dresser.

Cherry cheval dresser with incised lines and applied decorations, early 1900's. 48" wide, 21" deep, 84" high.

Oak cheval dresser with incised carving and applied decorations, early 1900's. 41" wide, 19" deep, 76" high.

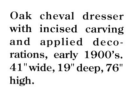

Mahogany stained birch (aniline dyed) arm chair with three cane panels, early 1900's. 25" arm to arm, 38" high.

Maple cheval dresser with incised carving, early 1900's. Maker's label on back reads: "Nelson-Matter, Grand Rapids, Michigan." 45" wide, 22" deep, 78" high.

CHEVAL MIRROR

When a tall swinging mirror is mounted on a frame that customarily stands on the floor so a viewer sees a full-length reflection, it is referred to as a cheval mirror.

Oak cheval mirror with applied decorations, early 1900's. 26" wide, 21" deep, 72" high.

CHIFFOROBE

A double-duty bedroom unit with drawers on one side and a door on the other that encloses a hanging place for garments is a chifforobe. This combination wardrobe-dresser was needed in the early 1900's when many homes did not have closets. One company produced such pieces under the brand name Chiffo-Robe while another used the name Dresserobe. Still another called this piece of furniture a "gentleman's chiffonier." Some have a full length mirror on the door and/or one above the chest portion.

Oriental V-matched and walnut veneered chifforobe with cedar lined section on left, 1940's. 34" wide, 19" deep, 62" high.

Oak chifforobe with waterfall top, 1940's. Originally finished in limed oak. Made by Lenoir Furniture Corporation; Lenoir, North Carolina. 41" wide, 21" deep, 71" high.

Oak Mission style chifforobe, 1920's. 45" wide, 20" deep, 69" high on door side, 74" high on mirror side.

Oak chiffonier with serpentine front, incised and applied decorations, hat box between upper drawers, swing mirror and claw feet, early 1900's. 39" wide, 22" deep, 75" high.

CHIFFONIER

Highboy is the current name antique dealers and collectors use for a narrow chest of drawers that early furniture catalogues listed as a chiffonier.

Oak chiffonier with serpentine front and swing mirror, early 1900's. 32" wide, 19" deep, 67" high.

Oak chiffonier with serpentine front, applied decorations, lions' heads on swing mirror frame, hat box to right of top drawers, and claw feet, early 1900's. 33" wide, 21" deep, 73" high.

Oak chiffonier with projection front top drawer, turned stiles, applied decorations and swing mirror, early 1900's. 35" wide, 19" deep, 66" high.

CHIFFORETTE

A bedroom unit with one or two drawers at the base and two doors above forms a chifforette. Behind the doors are sliding pull-out sections for storing personal possessions such as men's detachable collars, folded shirts, or undergarments.

Mahogany veneered chifforette with three drawers behind upper doors, 1920's. 34" wide, 20" deep, 48" high, 4" rail.

CHILDREN'S ITEMS

Articles for children include those which were designed for their actual use. These range from infant to youth sizes.

Child's oak rocker with grotesque face pressed into back rail, early 1900's. 15" arm to arm, 29" high.

Elm and maple pressed back, cane seat youth rocker, early 1900's. 19" arm to arm, 35" high.

Oak youth chair with horse design pressed into back rail, early 1900's. 16" arm to arm, 38" high.

Oak pressed back youth chair, early 1900's. 38" high.

Child's oak photographer's chair, early 1900's. 35" high.

Child's oak roll top desk with incised lines and applied decorations, 1920's. 26" wide, 17" deep, 37" high, 6" back rail.

Child's oak church bench, early 1900's. 48" wide, 15" deep, 27" high.

CHINA BUFFET

When a china cabinet and a sideboard are united so that characteristics of each are included, a china buffet results. The glass enclosed section can be in the "belly" of the piece or at one or both sides. A storage cabinet area is provided also.

Oak china buffet with claw feet and an enclosed showcase that has a lift top, early 1900's. 44" wide, 20" deep, 60" high.

Oak china buffet with convex glass and claw feet, 1920's. 46" wide, 19" deep, 52" high.

Oak china buffet with convex glass bow front, swell front base drawer and claw feet, early 1900's. 44" wide, 20" deep, 38" high.

Oak china buffet with swell top drawers, carved decorations and cabriole legs, early 1900's. 44" wide, 21" deep, 60" high.

Oak china buffet with swell drawer fronts, grotesques at top of pillars and leaded convex glass, early 1900's. 52" wide, 22" deep, 71" high.

CHINA CABINET OR CLOSET

This is a glass enclosed storage unit where china is displayed. The glass panels could be either straight, serpentine, convex or concave in shape. The convex with its outward swell is more common than the other types. In old catalogues, these were called bent glass.

Oak china cabinet with convex glass side panels, swell drawer front at base, applied decorations and claw feet, early 1900's. 49" wide, 15" deep, 74" high.

Oak china cabinet with convex glass side panels, early 1900's. 40" wide, 16" deep, 55" high.

Oak china cabinet with convex glass side panels and leaded glass in upper section, early 1900's. 43" wide, 14" deep, 62" high, 8" mirror.

Oak china cabinet with convex glass door and side panels, applied decorations and claw feet, early 1900's. 36" wide, 16" deep, 60" high, 13" mirror.

Oak china cabinet with convex glass door and side panels, grotesques at the top of the side pillars, applied decorations and carved animal feet, late 1800's or early 1900's. 48" wide, 18" deep, 70" high.

Oak china cabinet with convex glass side panels and claw feet, early 1900's. Made by West Michigan Furniture Co.; Holland, Michigan. 45" wide, 15" deep, 63" high, 4" rail.

Oak corner china cabinet with convex glass side panels and applied carving, early 1900's. 40" wide, 20" deep, 66" high.

Oak corner china cabinet with concave front glass panel, applied decorations and mirror and shelves at top, early 1900's. 40" wide, 20" deep, 58" high, 12" mirror.

Oak Mission style china cabinet, 1920's. 42" wide, 15" deep, 57" high, 2" rail.

Oak Mission style china cabinet with leaded glass in top panels, 1920's. 32" wide, 16" deep, 65" high.

Mahogany china cabinet with incised carving and grotesques at the top of stiles, early 1900's. 53" wide, 14" deep, 66" high.

Walnut veneered china cabinet with applied and incised carving and cabriole legs, 1920's. Part of a 9-piece dining room set sold by Landstrom of Rockford, Illinois (est. 1879). 39" wide, 18" deep bottom section; 36" wide, 14" deep top section; 75" high.

Mahogany china cabinet with broken pediment and applied decorations and beading, late 1930's or early 1940's. 37" wide, 15" deep bottom section; 34" wide, 13" deep top section; 77" high.

Orientalwood veneered china cabinet and selected hardwoods with applied decorations, late 1920's. 37" wide, 15" deep, 62" high, 5" rail.

China cabinet with V-matched Orientalwood and burl walnut veneer, 1930's. Part of a 9-piece dining room set. 36" wide, 15" deep, 68" high.

Mahogany china cabinet with waterfall top, 1940's. 33" wide, 14" deep, 64" high.

Mahogany corner cabinet with broken pediment, late 1940's. Made by Thomasville Chair Company. 30" wide, 15" deep, 79" high.

CHROMIUM

Chromium or chrome is a hard, metallic chemical element used in electroplating alloy steel. Chrome was used to make some of the furniture produced from the 1920's through the 1950's.

Porcelain top breakfast set with chromium legs on chairs and table, 1950's. 42" x 32", 32" high, 21" extension.

CLOCK

Most of the mantel, shelf or wall clocks found in the catalogues of the early 1900's could be purchased in either oak or walnut. As the century progressed, oak predominated. Many clocks featured die pressed designs on their cases.

Oak Ansonia "Queen Elizabeth" 8-day wall clock with time and strike, late 1800's or early 1900's. 14" wide, 38" high.

Oak Sessions shelf clock, 1920's. 8-day, time and strike. 15" wide, 23" high. Oak clock shelf with mirror in the center and incised designs, 1920's. 24" wide, 7" deep, 10" high.

COLONIAL STYLE

Furniture manufacturers copied and intermixed styles indiscriminately. In the 1920's this eclectic practice gave rise to furniture with scroll legs, columns and mirror supports. Manufacturers called their product "colonial furniture" although it really had Empire features from the 1815–1840 period and does not relate to the styles prevalent in this nation's colonial period prior to 1776. There were factories, however, that made quality copies of furniture found in wealthy colonial homes of the seventeenth and eighteenth centuries. These carefully constructed reproductions, rather than those of the 1920's, realistically deserve the name "colonial furniture."

Oak china cabinet, made in the colonial style, with scroll feet and convex glass in door and side panels, 1920's. 38" wide, 15" deep, 58" high, 3" rail.

Oak Gilbert shelf clock, 1920's. 8-day, time and strike with applied decorations and incised carving. 15" wide, 5" deep, 22" high.

Circassian walnut colonial style bedroom set from a 1915–1916 furniture catalogue that includes bed, dresser, chiffonier, dressing table and chair, desk table, suit chair and two rockers.

COMB CASE

This was a wall receptacle, sometimes accompanied by a mirror, that held combs and other grooming aids. Prior to the introduction of plumbing, it hung near a shelf or table that held the wash basin and pitcher.

Oak comb case with mirror and incised designs, 1920's. 12" wide, 2" deep, 20" high.

Oak washstand commode with bow front, applied decorations and attached towel bar rack, early 1900's. 34" wide, 21" deep, 55" high.

COMMODE (see Washstand Commode)

A commode was comprised of a combination of drawers and doors. The chamber set that was stored in this bedroom piece included the wash bowl, pitchers for heated and cold water, a toothbrush holder, a pot for nocturnal use and a lidded slop jar. Those that were called toilet (an early catalogue term for "mirror") washstands had a mirror in the back. Research in late 1920's catalogues showed that individual washstands were no longer prominently featured because by that time many homes had their water piped in.

Oak washstand commode with bow front, serpentine sides and applied decorations, early 1900's. 34" wide, 20" deep, 27" high, 4" splash back.

Oak half-commode or somnoe, 1920's. 16" wide, 15" deep, 29" high.

Bird's-eye and curly maple veneered washstand commode with serpentine drawers and attached towel bar rack, early 1900's. 32" wide, 19" deep, 53" high.

Oak washstand commode with attached towel bar rack, 1920's. 32" wide, 17" deep, 54" high.

Maple washstand commode with ogee top drawer, serpentine base and attached swing mirror and towel bar, early 1900's. 36" wide, 18" deep, 76" high.

Oak washstand commode with attached swing mirror, spoon carving and incised lines, late 1800's or early 1900's. 29" wide, 16" deep, 66" high.

COUCH

Couch was a term, found in catalogues during the first decade of the twentieth century, to denote what is currently called a fainting couch. Often it had tufted upholstery, a rounded head rest and a surface approximately 78" long. At times its frame was made of thoroughly seasoned hardwood, veneered with highly figured quarter sawed oak, finished in a rich golden color and highly polished. Also seen was a bed type that expanded to 44" x 72". A wardrobe version had a top that lifted to reveal a storage space beneath.

Oak couch-bed with incised lines, early 1900's. 74" wide, 24" deep, 37" high.

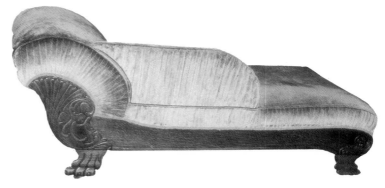

Oak couch with carved designs and claw feet, early 1900's. 76" wide, 31" high.

COUNTER DESK

Merchants frequently kept their accounts in a desk that sat on top of a counter. Sometimes this type of desk was distributed by companies, such as J &P Coats, Clark's or Merrick's, whose names were imprinted somewhere on the cabinet as an advertising ploy. Often an example included a combination desk-spool cabinet with a slanted lift lid and a series of six or more drawers.

Oak counter desk with lift lid and darkened tin panels on drawer fronts, early 1900's. 30" wide, 22" deep, 12" high at back.

CRADLE

A cradle is a baby's bed that moves on rockers or sways suspended from a supporting frame.

Oak cradle on frame, late 1800's or early 1900's. 39" long, 21" deep, 37" high headboard, 31" high footboard.

glass doors on top. Oak is the common wood choice. Today, the term pie shelf indicates that there is a separated space between the bottom and the top were food stuffs, such as pies, may be placed to cool and to be cut. During the 1930's and 1940's available cabinets or cupboards stood on legs.

Oak kitchen cabinet base with storage bin that opens, 1920's. 30" wide, 17" deep, 31" high.

CRAFTSMAN FURNITURE (see Stickley, Gustav)

Gustav Stickley, influenced by the English Arts and Crafts Movement, sought to escape the Victorian Era furniture produced from about 1840 to 1900. This style was overly ornamental and made predominately of the dark woods walnut, mahogany and rosewood. Stickley's wood choice was oak. For two years, Stickley experimented to perfect his style of severe, strong, straight-lined furniture often with obvious mortise and tenon joints. Some examples of these pieces, which he brand named "Craftsman," were exhibited at the Grand Rapids, Michigan Furniture Exposition in 1900.

CUPBOARD

The terms *cupboard* and *cabinet* are frequently used interchangeably because both serve as storage units. Sometimes a cupboard is considered a built-in architectural feature only whereas a free-standing version is called a cabinet. A closed type has wooden doors while an open cupboard refers to the absence of doors or to glass enclosed shelves which permit the contents to be seen. Cupboards vary greatly in both size and style. There are types that fit into corners as well as those that line up flat against walls. Some have drawers. Early century catalogues describe a projection base which is currently referred to as a *step back*. A straight front is straight up and down and usually has a closed base with two parallel drawers and two

Ash two-piece stepback cupboard, early 1900's. 44" wide, 19" deep, 79" high.

Oak cupboard with applied decorations, early 1900's. 39" wide, 15" deep, 80" high.

Oak two-piece cupboard, early 1900's. 41" wide, 24" deep top, 14" deep base, 83" high.

Oak stepback cupboard with applied decorations, early 1900's. 38" wide, 22" deep, 86" high.

CYLINDER DESK

A cylinder desk features a quarter-round, continuous hood that moves up and down in grooves to provide a solid, not a flexible, cover for the writing surface. Those constructed of oak and ash were found in the catalogues of the 1890's and early 1900's.

Oak cylinder desk with oak leaf inscribed at corners of cylinder, late 1800's or early 1900's. 41" wide, 22" deep, 46" high.

Oak cylinder desk with projection top drawer, incised lines and mirror and compartment on the top, late 1800's or early 1900's. 33" wide, 23" deep, 67" high.

CYLINDER SECRETARY

A secretary is a desk, usually with a series of drawers below the writing surface and a bookcase above. A cylinder secretary has a quarter-round, continuous hood that moves up and down in grooves to expose or cover the writing area. As was the case with cylinder desks, these secretaries were pictured in late 1800's and early 1900's catalogues.

Oak cylinder secretary with spoon carving, late 1800's or early 1900's. 39" wide, 22" deep, 86" high.

Oak cylinder desk with projection top drawer, applied decorations and hand carved designs on top drawer, late 1800's or early 1900's. 33" wide, 21" deep, 49" high.

DAVENPORT

A davenport is a large upholstered couch or sofa with a single or multi-cushioned seat. Bed davenports, named "Automatic" and "Unifold" were advertised in 1912 catalogues. Made of quarter-sawed oak, they had plain lines with a fumed finish. In 1922 a Kroehler brand "Daveno" could be purchased. One type could be pulled out to 60", while another measured 84". Davenport or sofa beds retain their useful quality. A 1952–1953 catalogue presented a sofa sleeper 54" wide and 75" long. A studio couch made a 58" x 72" bed or twin beds, each 29" x 72". One sofa sleeper included a generous size storage compartment.

Davenport with loose cushions, 1920's. 75" wide, 32" high.

DENTAL CABINET

Cabinets with drawers and doors where a dentist kept his tools and supplies are now being used by some homemakers. Many woods were used in their construction, with oak and mahogany being the dominant ones. Some combination metal and porcelain ones from the 1920 era are available.

Oak dental cabinet, 1920's. 36" wide, 13" deep, 44" high.

Oak dental cabinet with railing at the top, early 1900's. Made by the Harvard Company; Canton, Ohio. 25" wide, 19" deep, 55" high, 9" rail.

DEPRESSION ERA FURNITURE

(see Bedroom Suite, Parlor Set and Dining Room Set)

This refers to furniture made during an economically depressed period that the United States experienced from 1929 through the 1930's. Some examples of this style of furniture continued to be catalogued into the late 1950's. This furniture was characterized by the waterfall front, the extensive use of inlay work, imported veneers and copies of period pieces. The less expensive borax type furniture was often painted, artificially grained and stenciled. Veneerite, a paper strip that resembled inlay, was used for decoration. The chest of drawers pictured is an excellent example of a borax piece that is artificially designed in its entirety.

A borax chest of drawers with router designs, painted lines and artificial grain, 1930's. 32" wide, 17" deep, 47" high, 7" rail.

Bleached mahogany waterfall front cedar chest, 1930's. Marked "Roos Chest; Forest Park, Illinois." 44" wide, 19" deep, 21" high.

DESK

A desk is comprised of a writing or work surface, drawers, and storage compartments. Desks can range from simple table types to elaborate secretaries. The latter varieties, of oak or ash and with cylinder or fall fronts, have glass enclosed bookcase tops. They were illustrated in the late 1800's and early 1900's furniture catalogues. Also appearing in the early twentieth century were oak versions, frequently found in the parlor or library, that had fall fronts with open or glass enclosed book storage provisions at the base. Other fall fronts with single or double drawers beneath the desk area and supported by long legs were called lady's desks. Some had a bureau base composed of three drawers. Roll tops, which were most frequently found in offices or stores, and the desk-bookcase combina-

tion, were popular during the early century period. As the 1920's and 1930's approached, the Governor Winthrop desk and its fall-front secretary counterpart gained popularity. Pictured examples of these can be seen in *Furniture of the Depression Era* by Robert W. and Harriett Swedberg. These desks were predominately mahogany veneered, finished naturally or stained. There were, however, some painted versions.

Oak lady's desk with two parallel drawers above drop front, 1920's. 30" wide, 17" deep, 57" high.

Oak lady's desk with applied decorations and lower shelf, early 1900's. 26" wide, 14" deep, 48" high.

Oak lady's desk with swell drawers, carved designs and mirror top, cabriole legs and claw feet, early 1900's. 29" wide, 14" deep, 55" high.

Oak fall front desk with cabriole legs, early 1900's. 30" wide, 16" deep, 41" high.

Mahogany fall front desk with inlaid designs, 1930's. 34" wide, 18" deep, 42" high.

Oak lady's desk with applied decorations and mirror top, early 1900's. 28" wide, 15" deep, 47" high.

Ribbon mahogany and maple fall front desk, 1920's. 33" wide, 18" deep, 40" high.

Fall front desk, sometimes called "Sheboygan." Swell drawers, applied decorations, carved grotesque mirror supports and claw feet. Early 1900's, 32" wide, 14" deep, 70" high.

Oak fall front desk with bookcase section, early 1900's. 38" wide, 16" deep, 54" high.

Walnut veneered and selected hardwoods hotel desk with applied decorations. 26" wide, 17" deep, 30" high, 4" rail.

Oak desk, china cabinet and cupboard combination with cabriole legs, early 1900's. 46" wide, 15" deep, 64" high, 13" mirror.

Fall front desk with incised and applied decorations and glass enclosed bookcase bottom, early 1900's. 31" wide, 16" deep, 60" high.

Ash fall front desk and wardrobe combination, early 1900's. 52" wide, 15" deep, 70" high.

Oak fall front secretary with carved design on drop lid and bookcase top, early 1900's. 38" wide, 19" deep, 83" high.

Oak table top desk with compartment top, early 1900's. 35" wide, 26" deep, 56" high.

Mahogany desk, china cabinet combination with desk behind top center drop front drawer, 1920's. 52" wide, 16" deep, 77" high.

Ash fall front secretary with bookcase top, early 1900's. 44" wide, 18" deep, 94" high.

V-matched Orientalwood and zebrano veneered fall front secretary, 1930's. 28" wide, 15" deep, 68" high.

DINETTE SET (see Breakfast Set)

A smaller drop leaf or extension table with additional leaves and with four chairs was called a dinette or breakfast set. Since breakfast nooks were popular in the 1920's, two benches sometimes replaced the chairs in these cozy eating areas. Many sets were made of oak, left with the natural wood exposed. Others were painted. Some were hand painted or stenciled with floral, geometric or other designs. Shading or a strip of color sometimes occurred.

Introduced in the 1930's were stainproof porcelain-top tables with drop leaves. The base and the accompanying chairs were of oak. "Even the tops on oak sets are such perfect reproductions of the natural wood that you can hardly tell them apart," was the description of these porcelain table tops found in a 1933 Montgomery Ward catalog.

By the 1950's some dinette tables featured chrome legs. Their tops were either plastic or porcelain. Since styles remain the same over a period of years, breakfast sets in solid oak, popular in the 1920's and 1930's, with a table and four chairs, were still available through 1950 furniture catalogs.

Oak dinette set with painted designs on chair back and table top, 1940's. The set consists of a table and four chairs. Chair — 33" high. Table — 43" x 32", 29" high.

Oak dinette set consisting of a table and four chairs (one of which is not pictured), 1940's. Chair — 37" high. Table — 33" x 44", 31" high with two 9" leaves.

DINING ROOM SET

"A strikingly handsome nine-piece dining room suite" was advertised in the 1908 Sears, Roebuck Catalogue for $62.35. Their competitors, Sears stated, sold comparable oak sets for $90.00 to $100.00. A round top pedestal extension table, six chairs, a "buffet sideboard" with two glass enclosed doors and a china cabinet with "swell double thick bent glass ends and front" were included. Hand carved claw feet were present on all of the pieces. Although the set was made of solid oak, it was "finished in a perfect imitation of highly-figured quarter sawed oak."

Examples of fumed oak sets are difficult to find because many of them have been stripped of the dark finish. The set pictured in this section with its original, aged look gives one an excellent view of how dark the sets could be.

The use of a combination of walnut and Orientalwood veneers exemplifies the mannner in which woods were combined in the 1930's. The rounded waterfall fronts were stylish.

A pictured set made of selected hardwoods stained walnut was purchased new in 1937. A draw table featured a leaf at each end that could be pulled down to slide under the table top when not in use.

Walnut, Orientalwood and zebrano veneered nine-piece dining room set, early 1940's. Host chair — 22" arm to arm, 35" high. Side chair — 35" high. Extension table — 54" x 40", 31" high. Buffet — 59" wide, 19" deep, 41" high. China cabinet — 33" wide, 15" deep, 64" high.

Oak nine-piece dining room set with fumed oak finish, almost black with age, 1920's. Marked "Made in Grand Rapids" on the back of the server. Host chair — 23" arm to arm, 44" high. Side chair — 41" high. Dining extension table — 48" diameter. Buffet — 54" wide, 25" deep, 37" high. Server — 45" wide, 19" deep, 49" high. China cabinet — 48" wide, 16" deep, 63" high.

Walnut veneered eight-piece dining room set with applied decorations on table and buffet, late 1920's. Buffet — 65" wide, 22" deep, 39" high. Table — 59" x 41", 31" high. Host chair — 23" arm to arm, 37" high. Side chair — 37" high.

Walnut veneered and walnut stained selected hardwoods eight-piece dining room set, 1937. Host chair — 29" arm to arm, 43" high. Five side chairs — 40" high. Table — 62" x 38", 32" high with 17" draw leaves. Buffet — 66" wide, 20" deep, 38" high.

Oak drop leaf extension table, early 1900's. 42" x 23", 30" high with two 13" leaves.

Oak seven-piece dining room set with incised designs on chair backs and table apron, 1930's. Six slip seat chairs — 36" high. Table — 49" x 35", 32" high with two 10" leaves.

DINING ROOM TABLE

Oak round extension tables have seen continuing popularity in the twentieth century. Other versions of oak are the rectangular or square extension style and some kinds of drop leaf tables.

Right: Maple extension table that was originally artificially grained oak, early 1900's. It has five leaves, lions' heads on base of pedestal, and claw feet. 46" diameter, 30" high.

Oak extension table with split pedestal and paw feet, early 1900's. 45" diameter, 30" high.

Oak extension table with pedestal base and paw feet, early 1900's. 42" diameter, 30" high.

Oak extension table with four 13" leaves, lions' heads on legs, and paw feet, early 1900's. 45" diameter, 30" high.

DRESSER (see Princess Dresser)

A dresser is a chest of drawers, usually with a mirror. Elm, oak and ash varieties were made during the early decades of the twentieth century although birch, bird's-eye maple and mahogany examples could also be purchased. As the Depression Era approached, veneered dressers achieved popularity and their use continued through the 1940's. The 1950's featured the straight lined, wider dressers, called double or triple, that were finished quite often in limed oak or blond satinwood. A selection of woods including magnolia, gum, hackberry, larchwood, avodire and walnut was available.

Oak extension table with center supporting leg, early 1900's. 43" x 43", 30" high.

Oak three drawer chest, 1920's. 40" wide, 18" deep, 32" high.

Oak dresser with applied decorations, spoon carving, incised lines, decks and swing mirror, late 1800's or early 1900's. 39" wide, 18" deep, 80" high.

Ash dresser with incised lines, flower designs and swing mirror, early 1900's. 40" wide, 19" deep, 77" high.

Oak combination dresser, commode and desk with applied decorations and swing mirror, early 1900's. 48" wide, 20" deep, 80" high.

Oak dresser with applied decorations and swing mirror, early 1900's. 42" wide, 20" deep, 78" high.

Oak dresser with serpentine front, applied decorations and swing mirror, early 1900's. 45" wide, 21" deep, 74" high.

Oak dresser with serpentine front and grotesque designs on swing mirror supports, early 1900's. 38" wide, 20" deep, 70" high.

Oak dresser with serpentine front, applied decorations and swing mirror, early 1900's. 42" wide, 20" deep, 72" high.

Bird's-eye maple and maple dresser with swell top drawers and swing mirror, 1920's. 40" wide, 19" deep, 66" high.

Bleached and ribbon stripped mahogany chest of drawers, late 1920's. Part of a three-piece bedroom set (bed and dresser not pictured). 34" wide, 18" deep, 51" high.

Walnut vanity with swing mirror, carved fruit pulls, applied and incised decorations, 1940's. A selection from the Lillian Russell line made by Abernathy Furniture. 47" wide, 18" deep, 66" high.

DRESSING TABLE (see Vanity Table)

A table with a mirror or mirrors at which a woman sat to comb her hair and apply cosmetics is called a dressing or vanity table.

Walnut veneered vanity with adjustable side mirrors, 1920's. 48" wide, 19" deep, 69" high.

Oak vanity with adjustable side mirrors, 1920's. 38" wide, 18" deep, 55" high.

Oak vanity dresser with two hat boxes, applied decorations and swing mirror, early 1900's. 56" wide, 22" deep, 78" high.

Oak deep well vanity with adjustable side mirrors, serpentine front and applied decorations, early 1900's. 46" wide, 22" deep, 75" high.

F

FAINTING COUCH (see Couch)

Fainting couch is the current term for an elongated seat, usually with a raised, rounded pillow-like end on which one could rest ones head when reclining. Furniture catalogues from the early 1900's referred to this piece merely as a couch.

Oak fainting couch with tufted upholstered seat and back, applied and incised decorations, early 1900's. 67" wide, 24" deep, 36" high.

FILE CABINET

An office piece with multiple drawers for filing cards, folders and important papers is a file cabinet. Oak ones are popular for home use at the present time.

Five-piece sectional oak file cabinet, early 1900's. 33" wide, 17" deep, 52" high.

Single pedestal oak file cabinet, early 1900's. 18" wide, 29" deep, 53" high.

FIREPLACE SCREEN

This screen was placed in front of a fireplace to ward off the direct heat from the hearth. Some were adjustable in height. Screens could consist of a wooden frame with fancy needlework or tapestry inserts. Other materials could be used as well.

Six-piece stacking oak file cabinet bookcase, early 1900's. 34" wide, 16" deep, 60" high.

Mahogany framed fireplace screen with a garden scene oil painting on pictured side and Oriental scene on the reverse, 1920's. 32" wide, 37" high.

Oak framed fireplace screen with tapestry covering, early 1900's. 30" wide, 39" high.

GAME TABLE

As the name implies, games are played on a table of this type. Many fold. One form is hinged so that the top will fold over on itself to make a double top surface. Alternately, the portion that folds can stand up against the wall. This saves space when the table is not in use. A similar table was widely used in the nineteenth century and regained popularity again in the 1930's. Oak examples are scarce.

Oak game table with scooped out troughs for poker chips or coins at each end and applied beading, early 1900's. Top is on pins and can be raised and rotated to the left to cover the gambling part for conversion into a common lamp table. 36" x 36", 29" high.

Mahogany veneered and mahogany stained selected hardwoods game table, 1940's. 30" wide, 15" deep, 28" high, 15" drop leaf.

GOVERNOR WINTHROP DESK

Governor Winthrop is a name associated with a Chippendale style fall front desk that opens to expose document compartments, small drawers and pigeon holes in back of the writing surface. A series of long drawers is in the base. Puritan John Winthrop headed the Massachusetts Bay Colony after his arrival from England in 1630. Both his namesake son and grandson were governors of Connecticut. The latter, John III, died in 1707. The English cabinet-maker Thomas Chippendale was born in 1718, so these government leaders did not own such desks. It is merely a prestigious name that has been given to this style.

Right: Tiger maple Governor Winthrop fall front secretary, late 1930's. 30" wide, 15" deep, 76" high.

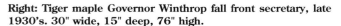

HALL MIRROR

This mirror was usually found in an oak frame with carving or applied decorations and hooks for hanging hats and coats. The larger variety was often part of a two-piece set that included a separate lift lid base. In early catalogues, the buyer could choose a two-piece set or either the individual top or base section. This probably explains why so many of the hall mirrors are available without the benches.

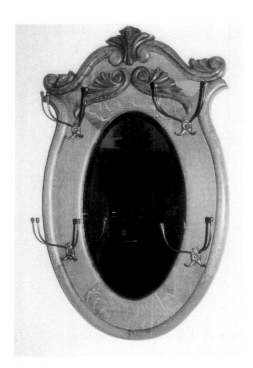

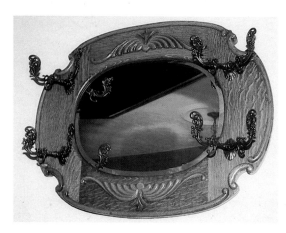

Oak hall mirror with applied decorations, early 1900's. 31" x 25".

Oak hall mirror with applied decorations, early 1900's. 24" x 38".

Oak hall mirror with applied decorations, early 1900's. 32" x 22".

Oak rectangualr hall mirror, 1920's. 32" x 21".

HALL TREE

A hall tree was usually located in the entry way where those who came into a home could hang their hats and coats. Most had mirrors and a lift lid storage box for articles of clothing and footwear such as scarves, mittens, woolen hats and boots. Umbrella holders with metal drip pans at the base were quite often an integral part of this piece.

Oak hall tree designed by Tomlin Cabinet Making Company, Maysville, Kentucky, with applied decorations and incised designs, 1893. Made and signed by Robert Mitchell Company, Cincinnati, Ohio as a wedding gift for Wadsworth Clark for his newly built home on West 3rd Street, Maysville. 46" wide, 18" deep, 77" high.

Oak two-part "hall tree" with applied decorations and side pillars, early 1900's. Bench with lift lid — 36" wide, 19" deep, 37" high. Hall mirror with four hat hooks — 34" wide, 33" high.

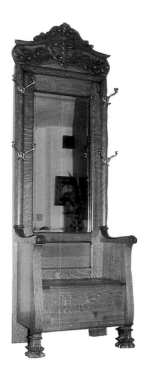

Oak hall tree with lift lid bench, incised lines and applied decorations, early 1900's. 29" wide, 17" deep, 78" high.

Oak hall tree with lift lid bench, applied decorations, early 1900's. 36" wide, 16" deep, 84" high.

Oak hall tree with lift lid bench, applied decorations, and paw feet, early 1900's. 28" wide, 17" deep, 90" high.

Oak hall tree with lift lid bench and applied decorations, early 1900's. 31" wide, 17" deep, 78" high.

Oak hall tree with applied decorations and metal umbrella holders, 1920's. 23" wide, 16" deep, 77" high.

Oak corner hall tree with lift lid bench and applied decorations, 1920's. 27" wide, 20" deep, 75" high.

Oak hall tree with applied decorations and arms to hold umbrellas, early 1900's. 27" wide, 13" deep, 82" high.

Hard rock maple nest of tables made by Heywood-Wakefield, late 1940's or early 1950's. 21" wide, 15" deep, 25" high for largest one.

HEYWOOD-WAKEFIELD COMPANY

In 1826, Levi Heywood began making wooden chairs in Gardner, Massachusetts. In 1874, Heywood Brothers and Company marketed reed and rattan furniture. Meanwhile, Cyrus Wakefield established his Rattan Works in South Reading, Massachusetts in 1855. These rival companies merged in 1897 under the name Heywood Brothers and Wakefield Company and grew to become the world's largest producers of wicker furniture. Later the name became Heywood-Wakefield Company. In the 1930's wicker gradually went out of vogue but interest in the ornate Victorian styles returned in the 1960's. Heywood-Wakefield's Wood Furniture Division closed in 1979. It was in the late 1940's and early 1950's that the company produced a line of furniture, including desks, china cabinets, high chairs and occasional tables made of rock maple. Most of these pieces were impressed with their trademark which consisted of a circle enclosing the company name and the words "established 1826." An eagle was also a part of the Heywood-Wakefield mark.

Hard rock maple lamp table made by Heywood-Wakefield, 1950's. 21" wide, 21" deep, 26" high.

Hard rock maple end table by Heywood-Wakefield, 1950's. 30" wide, 21" deep, 22" high.

Hard rock maple china cabinet by Heywood-Wakefield, 1950's. Base section — 50" wide, 19" deep, 32" high. Top section — 46" wide, 14" deep, 26" high.

Hard rock maple corner table made by Heywood-Wakefield, 1950's. 32" wide, 32" deep, 22" high.

Hard rock maple knee hole desk, 1950's. 44" wide, 18" deep, 29" high.

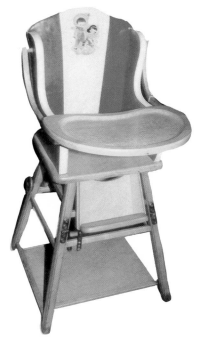

Oak chiffonier with serpentine front, applied decorations and swing mirror, early 1900's. 32" wide, 21" deep, 46" high, 24" mirror.

Hard rock maple high chair, go cart combination by Heywood-Wakefield, 1950's. 18" wide tray, 42" high.

HIGHBOY (see Chiffonier)

Furniture manufacturers in the early 1900's called a tall chest of drawers a chiffonier. Most antique dealers and collectors currently refer to this piece of furniture as a highboy even though it does not resemble the classical examples or fit the definition of the traditional highboy.

HIGHBOY, PERIOD STYLE

The classical, period style highboy, manufactured in the seventeenth and eighteenth centuries, was a tall chest of drawers, often in two sections. The base, known as a lowboy, resembled a table with long legs. Often it included a few drawers. Starting around the 1920's and continuing for several decades some of these period pieces have been accurately reproduced.

Oak chiffonier, 1920's. 33" wide, 17" deep, 47" high, 6" rail.

Walnut veneered highboy with shell on knees of cabriole legs, 1930's. 33" wide, 20" deep, 59" high.

HIGH CHAIR

A baby's chair with an attached tray and tall legs was where a small child sat at mealtime. Old catalogues called the tray a table and the entire unit a table chair. Painted golden and red ones were illustrated in a 1901 catalogue. They were also available in elm, ash or oak. A 1929 catalogue advertised three kinds of high chairs. One was constructed of hardwood, finished in a golden gloss. The second was finished in rich ivory enamel with an artistic transfer on the back panel. Its blue enameled table could swing to the back of the chair. The last is like the latter example except that it had a handy removable aluminum tray that could be lifted off for cleaning.

Oak pressed back high chair, early 1900's. 15" wide, 42" high.

Oak Mission style high chair, early 1900's. 17" wide, 20" deep, 40" high.

HIGH CHAIR AND GO CART COMBINATION

A high chair that folds down so the wheels touch the floor and a push handle emerges at the back is one example of high chair and go cart combination. Today this push portion with wheels would be called a stroller.

Right: Oak high chair, go cart combination with cane seat and pressed back, early 1900's. 17" wide, 42" high.

Hard rock maple high chair, go cart combination, 1950's. Made by Heywood-Wakefield. 18" wide, 41" high.

Oak Seller's kitchen cabinet with porcelain working surface and pull down tambour door, 1920's. 41" wide, 26" deep, 70" high.

HOOSIER CABINET

The Hoosier Manufacturing Company located at New Castle, Indiana produced kitchen cabinets. As early as 1902, the name was mentioned in catalogues. *Hoosier cabinet* became the generic name for a kitchen cabinet that often included a pull-out work space, cupboard storage, drawers, flour bins, sifters and other work and step-saving conveniences. Other well-known company and brand names of kitchen cabinets included Greencastle, Boone, Sellers, Wilson, Hawkeye, and Nappanee.

By 1927, the Sears, Roebuck catalogue asked, "Why not let it [the cupboard] work for you in your house as you pay for it? A small down payment and equally small payments every month now put this cabinet within reach of every home. Days of kitchen drudgery can now be lightened." If a man bought it for his wife, it would be "the happiest surprise of her life!" Buying with a little bit down and monthly payments was a new way to attract customers.

Ward-Bilt Kitchen Cabinets of the early 1930's were constructed of selected hardwoods finished in enamel colors of white, ivory, green or two tone ivory with green doors. One cabinet was available in selected oak finished golden. As the 1940's terminated, the Hoosier cabinet was on its way out. Built-in cupboards were becoming prevalent.

Oak "Hoosier type" kitchen cabinet with wooden working surface, 1920's. 40" wide, 27" deep, 69" high.

Oak Seller's kitchen cabinet with porcelain working surface and pull down tambour door, 1920's. 41" wide, 27" deep, 67" high.

Limed oak Napanee kitchen cabinet in three sections, late 1940's. Tag says it was made by "Napanee Coppes, Inc.; Napanee, Indiana." 76" wide, 70" high.

Oak "Hoosier type" kitchen cabinet with porcelain working surface, pull down tambour door and dome top, 1930's. Marked in black on the back is "oyster white" as the original factory color. 40" wide, 26" deep, 74" high.

HOSTESS WAGON (see Tea Cart)

A small, serving push-cart on wheels that had shelves for dishes, beverages or food is called by various names — tea cart, hostess wagon or tea wagon. They were found in abundance from the 1920's through the 1940's and were made of selected hardwoods, including oak, cherry and walnut, as well as mahogany and walnut veneers. Some were decorated with colorful Oriental hand-painted designs.

Mahogany hostess wagon with pull out handle, 1920's. 34" wide, 16" deep, 31" high.

HOTEL WASHSTAND

Mail order catalogues from the early 1900's picture hotel washstands and suggest they are primarily for use in hotel rooms. Both a mirror and a bar for holding towels were usually included. A commode base provided both drawer and cupboard space.

Oak hostess wagon with incised lines and applied decorations, late 1800's or early 1900's. 30" wide, 20" deep, 30" high.

Oriental designed hostess wagon with removable tray and pull out handle, 1920's. 26" wide, 17" deep, 29" high.

Oak hotel washstand with serpentine, projection top drawer, applied decorations and combination towel bar and mirror rack, early 1900's. 34" wide, 17" deep, 68" high.

Walnut and maple tea cart with removable glass tray, 1940's. 28" wide, 18" deep, 27" high.

ICE BOX

Refrigerator is the term generally used in mail order catalogues of the early 1900's rather than *ice box*. Food was stored in insulated compartments and a large block of ice was placed in the top section. When the air circulated and warm air rose, the cold air was forced down to cool the contents. The cycle was continuous. Many of the boxes are made of elm, but some are of ash or oak.

Oak three-door ice box, 1920's. 35" wide, 18" deep, 39" high.

Ash single door ice box with applied decorations, 1920's. 24" wide, 16" deep, 38" high.

ICE CHEST

Food and beverages were kept cold when a large block of ice was placed with them in an insulated, metal lined ice chest, usually from 25" to 33" in height with lift top covers. Five sizes were available, according to the 1907 Sears, Roebuck catalogue. Those made of elm had a "high gloss golden finish." Oak and ash varieties were also marketed.

Oak ice chest, 1920's. 33" wide, 21" deep, 32" high.

ICE CREAM PARLOR FURNITURE

Chairs and tables used in drug store soda fountain areas, in ice cream parlors, or in candy stores were called ice cream sets. Many versions of the chairs had hooped or heart backs of metal, a rounded seat and metal legs. The table tops were often made of oak, selected hardwoods, marble or a composition material. These sets as well as stools were listed in a 1915–1916 catalogue under the classification of wire furniture.

Ice cream table with oak top, 1920's. Table — 24" diameter, 31" high. Five piece set including four chairs (not pictured) — 34" high.

LARKIN SOAP MANUFACTURING COMPANY

John B. Larkin established a soap company in 1875 that, by 1892, became the Larkin Soap Manufacturing Company. It was located in Buffalo, New York. The company developed a club system that gave members who bought supplies, and urged friends to buy also, the opportunity to earn points that could be used to secure "Larkin Furniture." Other premiums from this mail order house included such accessory articles as rugs, silverware, curtains, linens, and lamps. It was also possible to acquire merchandise with a combination of cash and coupons. Some of the oak furniture was manufactured in Buffalo but a great deal came from factories elsewhere. It was shipped "knocked down" and full instructions were included so the recipient could assemble the article. How to care for Larkin pieces was described also. The following is a verbatim copy of an attached instruction sheet.

Helpful information. Atmospheric conditions and changes encountered by furniture while in transit &, often, in the home cause new wood to swell, so the doors & drawers bind & stick. In the winter the dry heat in the house will generally prove a sufficient remedy within a few weeks & it is better to avoid dressing down the wood, because it is designed to fit perfectly when dry. In the humidity of the summer, however, if the months when the house shall again be heated seem too distant to wait for a natural shrinkage, anyone with a good plane may with intelligent care dress the part that binds just enough to make action free. But never put the plane on drawers until first you have withdrawn them from the case, inverted them & examined lower-edge of front, also the tops of stationary rails between drawers, for possible excess of varnish which should be scraped off with knife or glass. Before planing a door-edge apply a screw driver to the hinge screws to make sure that they were driven quite in so the hinges entirely close, examine all four edges of door, particularly the hinged edge for excessive varnish. Often, lubrication of the bearing points with Sweet Home Soap is all that is required.

EVERY new piece of furniture should be given a liberal application of Larkin Furniture Polish to remove any chafing, scratches & the dust of travel.

Drawer pulls, casters & all trimmings if any, will be found, packaged in a drawer if any. Key will be found attached to outside of case.

To open a drawer that sticks. Place against the corner post of case at end of drawer, a small block of wood over a heavy pad of paper. Strike block a sharp blow with a hammer. Repeat this at each end alternately until drawer will open. Larkin, Buffalo, N.Y. Factory #19.

If you have any occasion to write us about it, mention this number without fail. Do not cause useless delay for inquiry, by neglecting this. Preserve all crating material until all possibility of reshipment of this article is past.

Larkin fall front oak desk with applied decorations and bookcase base, early 1900's. 30" wide, 12" deep, 62" high.

LIBRARY TABLE

Library tables were designed as a reading center where books, periodicals, or newspapers were available. Many of them had heavy curved pillars and scrolled feet. The outline of a lyre appeared on some. This was a revival of the Empire look of the early 1800's, but manufacturers at the turn of the century called the style "colonial," a misnomer. Some of these tables are cut down in height to serve as coffee tables. Tops were oval or rectangular and were commonly of oak veneer or artificially grained oak. A drawer and a base shelf were present. Mission examples were sturdy and straight and most were made of oak.

Oak library table with one drawer, early 1900's. 44" wide, 28" deep, 29" high.

Oak library table with cabriole legs and paw feet, early 1900's. 42" wide, 26" deep, 29" high.

Oak library table with one drawer, pillars and scroll feet, early 1900's. 36" wide, 24" deep, 30" high.

Oak library table with incised designs on drawer front, early 1900's. 36" wide, 23" deep, 29" high.

Oak Mission style library table, 1920's. 42" wide, 27" deep, 30" high.

Oak library table with bulbous legs, early 1900's. 42" wide, 28" deep, 29" high.

Oak library table with cabriole legs and paw feet, early 1900's. 42" wide, 28" deep, 30" high.

Limbert fumed oak desk, early 1900's. 33" wide, 16" deep, 43" high.

LIMBERT, CHARLES P.

The label for Limbert's products, branded into the wood, shows an artisan busy at a work table. The identifying words are "Limberts Arts Crafts Furniture Made in Grand Rapids and Holland" (Michigan). Much hand work was done on white oak, which was used exclusively, in the production of their plain-lined Mission style furniture. Some of the styles found in the furniture of early Dutch cabinet makers were incorporated into their furniture.

No carving or applied decorations were employed, and the only veneers found were on drawer bottoms and the backs of case pieces. Fumed finishes, resulting from exposure to ammonia vapors, were available as were others such as weathered, early English and golden oak. The company began operating in 1889 in Grand Rapids with Charles P. Limbert as president. Its Mission line was produced from approximately 1903 to 1917 when fashions changed and the pseudo "Colonial" style came into vogue.

Because the company did not wish to have its furniture confused with some of the poorly made Mission furniture of the time, the following proclamation of quality came from the office of the president:

> "All Cabinet Work from Limberts Arts and Crafts Workshop has Our Trade Mark branded into the Wood. This is a Means of Identification, a Guarantee of Excellence and the Acknowledgment We and Our Associates make that Limbert's Holland Dutch Arts and Crafts Furniture will give Absolute Satisfaction and that We stand Ready to Exchange or make Good any Piece that is Defective in any Way."

Impressed Limbert's label.

LIVING ROOM SUITE (or Parlor Suit)

Living room suites or parlor suits were available in matching sets that included a seat for several people such as a sofa or davenport, a divan or settee, which were small sofas, and various numbers and sizes of chairs. A rocking chair or platform rocker was often included.

An 1897 catalogue offered overstuffed parlor suits made up of a sofa, rocker, arm chair and two parlor chairs which were upholstered in a choice of cotton tapestry, crushed plush or silk tapestry. In catalogues from 1899 through 1905 birch three-piece parlor sets finished in mahogany were offered for sale. Also available were golden oak sets with upholstered back and seat. A 1906–1907 catalogue advertisement under parlor sets referred to their covering by saying, "Upholstered furniture — these goods are made by experienced finishers and upholsterers, not by boy labor and are first class in every respect. They are not of the 'Catalogue House' or 'Department Store' variety." These remarks were undoubtedly aimed at Montgomery Ward and Sears, Roebuck.

In the late 1800's and early 1900's, a parlor was set aside for special guests and held the family's best furniture. Women's magazines stated that the family was more important and the comfortable setting should be for their use, not reserved for visitors. For a time the names "parlor" and "living room" were used interchangeably. Around the early 1930's the term "living room" replaced "parlor" to describe the room and its furnishings. It was now a comfortable assembly center for the family, not the formal place to entertain guests such as the minister, the daughter's best beau, or relatives or friends seen only occasionally.

Two-piece mahogany parlor set with holly inlaid designs and pearl inserts, early 1900's. Love seat — 40" arm to arm, 21" deep, 35" high. Arm chair — 23" arm to arm, 34" high.

Two-piece upholstered living room set with grotesques on arm fronts, late 1920's or early 1930's. Sofa — 69" wide, 32" high. Tub or barrel chair — 28" arm to arm, 32" high.

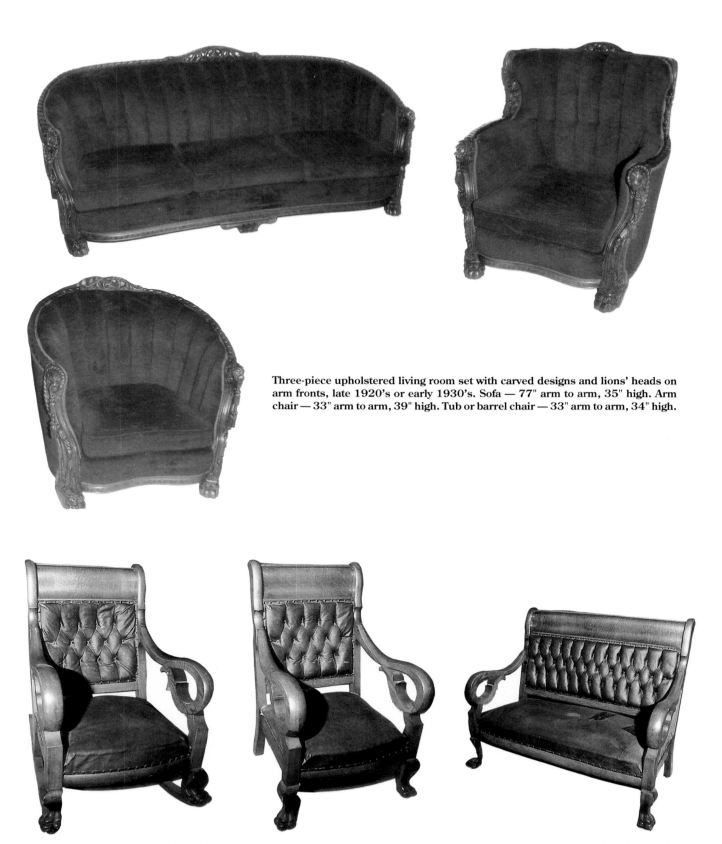

Three-piece upholstered living room set with carved designs and lions' heads on arm fronts, late 1920's or early 1930's. Sofa — 77" arm to arm, 35" high. Arm chair — 33" arm to arm, 39" high. Tub or barrel chair — 33" arm to arm, 34" high.

Three-piece oak parlor set with black leather seats and tufted backs, early 1900's. Rocker — 28" arm to arm, 39" high. Arm chair — 27" arm to arm, 42" high. Sofa — 51" arm to arm, 24" deep, 43" high.

MAGAZINE BASKET

Magazine basket, stand or rack are all names for receptacles to hold magazines. They often had handles for ease in moving and were handsomely finished in vivid lacquers with pretty floral designs. They varied in size from one to six pockets and were advertised as being capable of holding all standard size magazines. Stands were conveniently located on the floor near a chair or sofa where their contents were within easy reach of the reader.

Birch magazine rack with caned sides, 1940's. 15" wide, 10" deep, 29" high.

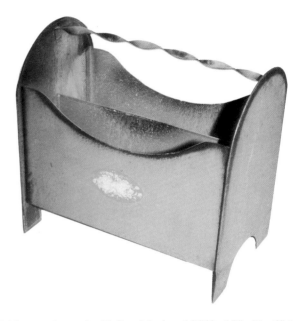

Metal magazine rack with floral design, 1930's. 13" wide, 8" deep, 13" high.

MARTHA WASHINGTON SEWING CABINET

A small storage unit for sewing needs that usually has three drawers and two five-cornered side pockets with hinged lift lids is called a Martha Washington sewing cabinet. They were often made of gumwood and finished in a brown mahogany or dull American walnut finish. More expensive ones could be constructed of hardwood veneers.

Cedar combination magazine rack and sewing stand, 1920's. 27" wide, 13" deep, 27" high.

Walnut Martha Washington sewing cabinet, 1940's. 29" wide, 14" deep, 30" high.

MEDICINE CABINET

A medicine cabinet usually hangs on the wall. It can hold medications, first aid equipment, and toiletries such as tooth brushes and paste. Some have mirrors.

Kitchen table with porcelain top and tubular metal legs, 1940's. 40" x 25", 31" high, 10" drop leaves.

Oak double door medicine cabinet, 1920's. 24" wide, 7" deep, 24" high.

METAL FURNITURE

Metal furniture traces its ancestry back to ancient times. Examples of antiquities fashioned of brass, bronze, and iron have been found and preserved.

In modern times, both brass and iron beds were factory made in the late 1800's. Brass beds continued to be made in the 1900's. Those of tubular steel were manufactured in the mid 1920's.

When the influence of Art Deco designs was felt from 1925 through the 1930's, metal furniture often wore a disguise. A metal bedroom set might be painted or artificially grained to resemble wood. The American designer Norman Bel Geddes advocated a trim, efficient look, with no excessive decoration. In addition to creating plans for the first streamlined ocean liner, Bel Geddes designed furniture for the Simmons Company, New York, N.Y. In 1935, this firm was advertised as the world's largest maker of furniture and bedding. A Bel Geddes metal bedroom set with black lacquer and chrome had a trim, simple-lined, almost streamlined appearance. It was displayed in Carson Pirie Scott's department store windows while the Century of Progress Exposition, held in Chicago in 1934, was attracting thousands of visitors to that city.

In the late 1940's, chrome and nickel-plated items were available. Smokers or smoking stands often reflected such flashy surfaces. Dinette sets with chrome legs and porcelain tops were manufactured in the 1950's.

Metal artificially grained bed with floral designs on headboard and footboard slats, 1920's. Marked "Built for Sleep Simmons Company." 54" wide, 48" high headboard, 32" high footboard.

Metal bed colored green with gilt accents that was featured in a 1915–1916 furniture catalogue. 54" wide, 52" high headboard, 40" high footboard.

Oak Mission fall front desk, early 1900's. 32" wide, 17" deep, 44" high.

Metal washstand with enamel bowl and pitcher, 1920's. 15" diameter, 31" high.

MISSION FURNITURE

Mission is the generic name for all the solid, straight lined, substantial, heavy oak furniture with obvious joinery that was manufactured from about 1900–1917. How did it acquire that title when Gustav Stickley, after being influenced by England's Arts and Crafts Movement of the late 1800's, experimented for two years before he exhibited his furniture at the Grand Rapids, Michigan Furniture Exposition in 1900? The name he registered with the United States government was "Craftsman."

There have been various theories suggested. Some say that Spanish monks worked with their converts many years to build small missions in the far west. Neither these religious leaders nor members of their parish were knowledgeable carpenters. As a result, their tables and benches were simply and often crudely made. Because this new furniture was severe and plain in its design, it reminded people of the benches the Spanish missionaries and their congregations made. Therefore, it earned the title "Mission." Some manufacturers added applied or cut out crosses to their products as if they supported this story of Mission's derivations.

Others declare that each piece of furniture has a purpose. A chair is to sit upon. A bed is the place to sleep. Each article has its own function — its reason for being. That's its mission; hence the name.

Interest in this plain-lined, structurally sound, functional furniture started to revive around 1970. Today, examples, especially those made by Gustav Stickley, are eagerly sought. His pieces have exceptionally high price tags.

MORRIS CHAIR

William Morris, one of the promoters of England's Arts and Crafts Movement, generally receives credit for developing the Morris Chair in the late 1800's. This chair that bears his name has loose seat and back cushions in a wooden frame. Its back is adjustable, thus allowing the user to sit erect or to recline if desired. Other recliners with brand names of Regal, Columbia and Hemco were featured and promoted as being as good as the Morris Chair, if not better. Examples were found in catalogues during the first twenty years of the 1900's.

Oak Morris type reclining chair, early 1900's. 31" arm to arm, 31" high.

MURPHY BED

This is the generic title that has been given to beds that fold up to resemble a free-standing cabinet. Mantel and upright folding beds were descriptive terms from catalogues from 1897 through the early years of the 1900's. The beds looked like mantels and had French beveled mirrors above the shelf. Their inside size usually measured 4' x 6'. Some had swell or paneled fronts. They were illustrated in catalogues until around 1916. Various versions of combination folding beds were available — bed and wardrobe; bed, writing desk, bookcase, and wardrobe; bed, bookcase and writing desk; and bed and dresser. Today the generic term Murphy bed is used to refer to all of these types.

MUSIC CABINET OR STAND

These small cabinets can hold tune sheets for music boxes, records for phonographs, or sheet music for musicians.

Oak music stand, early 1900's. 20" wide, 15" deep, 35" high.

Oak Murphy type bed with serpentine front, applied decorations, early 1900's. 54" wide, 20" deep, 52" high, 20" mirror.

Oak music cabinet with applied decoration and bevel mirror on top, 1920's. 21" wide, 15" deep, 40" high, 8" mirror.

NIGHT STAND

This bedroom piece usually occupied a space near the bed. It could be a table or could include a storage unit as well.

Walnut veneered night stand with paper banding around drawers imitating ebony and holly marquetry, 1930's. One of a pair. 19" wide, 15" deep, 29" high.

Oak marble top night stand, late 1800's or early 1900's. 17" wide, 16" deep, 34" high.

PARLOR SET OR SUIT (see Living Room Suite)

Parlor, meaning a formal room set aside for entertaining special guests, is now an obsolete term, replaced by the comfortable term *living room*.

Oak three-piece upholstered parlor set with incised designs, early 1900's. Settee — 36" arm to arm, 40" high. Arm chair — 25" arm to arm, 38" high. Platform rocker — 25" arm to arm, 38" high.

PEDESTAL

This term has various meanings. It can refer to a tall, narrow, often ornamental stand on which statues or plants are placed. It is also the central support on a table and can terminate with four legs, either plain or elaborate. At times, the two sides of a knee hole desk that house the drawers or cupboard areas are referred to as pedestals.

Quarter sawed oak pedestal with grotesque head on front upright, early 1900's. 12" square, 33" high.

Oak pedestal, early 1900's. 24" diameter, 29" high.

Oak pedestal with twisted pillar, early 1900's. 14" diameter, 36" high.

Quarter sawed oak triple pillar pedestal with claw feet, early 1900's. 14" diameter, 36" high.

PHONOGRAPH

After Thomas A. Edison invented the phonograph in 1877, its case grew in importance. At first, table models were available. Later, free standing examples were promoted. Early phonographs were hand wound with a crank. Eventually electricity provided the power. Edison called his "talking machine" his favorite invention. As a typical father might do, he quoted a child's poem when he recorded his first words. It was the verse, "Mary had a little lamb," written by Sara Josepha Hale, editor of *Godey's Lady's Book*.

Brunswick oak phonograph. Made by the Brunswick-Balke-Collender Co., 1920's. 23" wide, 23" deep, 50" high.

Edison oak phonograph, sold by M.L. Parker Co., Davenport, Iowa, 1917. 21" wide, 22" deep, 52" high.

Victor oak table model phonograph, 1920's. 13" wide, 15" deep, 8" high.

Mahogany Victrola phonograph, 1920's. Sold by Baxter Piano Co., Davenport, Iowa. 19" wide, 22" deep, 44" high.

PHOTOGRAPHER'S CHAIR

People frequently posed for studio portraits while sitting in a decorative chair, usually with a high back. Such fancy chairs received their name because they were used in this fashion.

Oak photographer's chair with twisted legs and applied decorations on back, early 1900's. 40" high.

Oak photographer's chair, early 1900's. 23" arm to arm, 34" high.

PHYFE, DUNCAN

The cabinetmaker, Duncan Phyfe, worked in New York City from approximately 1795 to 1847. Manufacturers copied his works in the 1900's. His tables frequently featured legs that curved out from a series of pedestals beneath the table. They had a floor-hugging sweep and their tips were capped with metal. His lyre back chairs and others with a carved top slat and modified cabriole legs were commonly reproduced to help form a dining room set. Such lines are graceful in appearance and were popular in the mid 1900's.

Mahogany stained Duncan Phyfe style side chair, 1940's. One of a set of four, 35" high.

Mahogany stained Duncan Phyfe style side chair with mahogany veneered lyre back, 1940's. One of a set of four, 33" high.

Duncan Phyfe drop leaf table made of mahogany veneered and
mahogany stained selected hardwoods, 1940's. 41" x 24", 30"
high, 16" drop leaves.

PIANO STOOL AND BENCH

A piano stool provided a place for a pianist to sit while
playing the piano. Most round ones can be adjusted in
height. Some of the revolving type have backs. Rectangular benches generally had a lift lid storage compartment in
the seat where music and song books were kept.

Maple piano stool with back and ball and claw feet, early 1900's.
36" high.

Oak piano stool with ball and claw feet, 1920's. 15" diameter.

Oak lift lid piano bench with cabriole legs and paw feet, 1920's.
36" wide, 15" deep, 20" high.

PIER MIRROR

Architecturally speaking, the wall space between windows and other openings is referred to as a pier. A tall, narrow, usually decorative mirror often occupied such a space and was, therefore, a pier mirror.

Oak pier mirror with marble shelf, incised designs and applied decorations, late 1800's or early 1900's. 29" wide, 9" deep, 87" high.

Oak and elm pie safe with round screened ventilation sections on each side, early 1900's. 41" wide, 16" deep, 53" high.

PIE SAFE

Housewives of yore often baked a batch of pies at one time. These freshly baked items were stored in a cupboard called a pie safe. Although most popular during the nineteenth century, these continued to be used during the first several decades of the twentieth century. In a 1901 catalogue pie safes are shown. These have tin panels punched with designs such as stars or circles. The perforations permitted air to circulate to retard molding and prevented rodents or flies from reaching the baked goods. Although poplar and ash were the wood choices at the time, many safes of oak, maple and pine were made during the early 1900's. Screening or punched board panels were sometimes used.

Oak planter, early 1900's. 82" wide, 14" deep, 29" high.

PLANTER

A planter with its growing vegetation adds color to a room. A large one can serve as a room divider. The one illustrated is made of oak and was retrieved from a school for nurses to enhance a hallway in a home.

PLATE RAIL

A wall shelf made to display ornamental plates is known as a plate rail. Often hooks for hanging decorative cups were a part of this rail.

Oak plate rail with mirrors in back and hooks for hanging cups, 1920's. 44" wide, 6" deep, 27" high.

Oak platform rocker with rolled veneer seat and applied decorations, early 1900's. 23" arm to arm, 41" high.

Oak plate rail with leaded glass door enclosing two compartments and provisions for hanging cups at bottom, early 1900's. 38" wide, 7" deep, 29" high.

PLATFORM ROCKER

In the late 1800's and early 1900's, various types of patented furniture became available. A rocker that moved back and forth on a platform or that had a spring action was one example. The resulting chairs did not creep across the floor, tilt back excessively, or have rockers that caused wear on carpets. There were people who were afraid to use ordinary rocking chairs because they might tilt too far back and topple over. Also, a sitter occasionally rocked off a porch and was injured. A patented form avoided these problems.

Oak pressed back platform rocker, late 1800's or early 1900's. 26" arm to arm, 48" high.

Oak pressed back platform rocker, early 1900's. 25" arm to arm, 43" high.

Oak coin operated player piano with leaded glass panels, early 1900's. Made by Peerless Piano Player Co., St. Johnsville, NY. 66" wide, 30" deep, 58" high.

PLAYER PIANO

A piano is a large, stringed percussion instrument a musician plays by using a keyboard. A built-in mechanism in a player piano depresses the keys automatically in response to signals on a perforated roll. Originally, a person sat and pumped up and down on two pedals to produce the sound. The words of songs were frequently printed on the revolving roll so that groups could participate in a fun sing-along around the piano. Rolls could be changed.

The illustrated example is a Mission oak Peerless Coin-Operated Player Piano which once occupied space in a public place such as a restaurant or a bar. Usually a nickel was inserted to play one roll. Made by the Peerless Piano Co., St. Johnsville, NY, it is electrified so pumping is not required. The three leaded glass panes light up as do two hanging lamps.

Polychrome frame, 1920's. 17" wide, 24" high.

POLYCHROME DECORATIONS

Polychrome decorations result with the application and blending of many colors on articles such as frames, mirrors and metal lamp columns and bases.

PRESSED BACK

A design that imitated carving was pressed into the backs of some chairs and other pieces of furniture with a metal die or mold. Sometimes a little carving was added to heighten the pattern. This type of chair was introduced in the catalogues of the 1890's and continued to be available during the first decade of the twentieth century. A chair made of oak, except for its elm seat, with a single press on its back was pictured in an 1894 catalogue. The catalogue also shows a pressed back rocker. These early catalogues had many names for such designs, including die cut, carved, embossed, hand carved, and carved. The term *pressed* was not found.

In 1897, double pressed backs, the term used now to indicate that there are designs on two parts of the back, were seen in rockers and chairs made of oak. Pressed back table chairs, now called high chairs, children's rockers, ladies' chairs which were referred to as misses' rockers, and office chairs were advertised. A 1901 catalogue shows the Man of the Wind design, a head with a mouth shaped as though blowing. A Ward's 1902 catalogue advertises straight chairs, office chairs and rockers that have "upper panels or panel backs richly and handsomely carved." One rocker was listed as "hand carved." In 1905, a dozen elm chairs with die cut carving could be purchased for $26.00 whereas a similar set in oak cost $43.00. By 1910, hardly any embossed back chairs or rockers were seen in the catalogues. After 1915, none were seen.

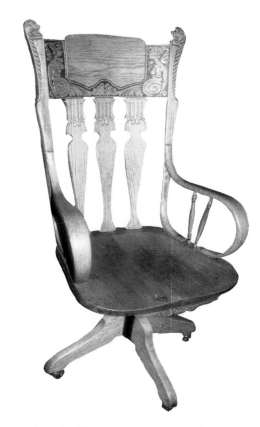

Oak pressed back office chair with mermaids on top rail, early 1900's. 25" arm to arm, 45" high. Below: close-up of mermaids on chair.

Maple double pressed back rocker with "Man of the Wind" on top rail, early 1900's. 25" arm to arm, 44" high.

PRESSED CANE

When cane purchased in pre-woven sheets is cut to fit an empty space in a chair, the wet sheet is pulled straight and taut and the ends are glued into an incised groove that outlines the gap. The woven sheet is held securely in place by measured pieces of spline that are forced into the router lines and glued. The soaked webbing tightens as it dries and a firm seat results.

Bird's-eye maple rocker with pressed cane seat, 1920's. 32" high.

PRINCESS DRESSER

A low, perhaps two drawer, dresser with a rather large, vertically elongated swing mirror, is called a princess dresser. Most have a dainty appearance. Perhaps this regal, diminutive look earned them the imaginative title *princess dresser.*

Oak princess dresser with bow or swell front and swing mirror, early 1900's. 30" wide, 20" deep, 68" high.

Oak princess dresser with serpentine front, applied decorations, swing mirror and cabriole legs, early 1900's. 34" wide, 19" deep, 70" high.

Oak princess dresser with serpentine front, decks, swing mirror and cabriole legs, early 1900's. 40" wide, 19" deep, 70" high.

PRISCILLA SEWING STAND

This portable sewing stand with hinged slant lids covering the two enclosed storage units has a handle across the top. It can be moved to a position beside a chair or near a sewing machine.

Walnut Priscilla sewing stand, 1920's. 15" wide, 12" deep, 24" high.

Mahogany Priscilla sewing stand, 1920's. 13" wide, 12" deep, 25" high.

 **R**

RADIO

Radio waves radiate out from a broadcasting station and a radio set changes them into sound waves so that listeners can hear the sounds. The Italian inventor, Guglielmo Marconi experimented with radio waves in 1895. The first commercial broadcast was aired in the United States in 1920 with music provided by phonograph records. The Harding-Cox presidential election returns were reported that same year, the first time such news was heard on the air. A listener had to wear earphones to hear the broadcast. By the mid-1920's, separate loud speakers replaced the earphones and everyone in the room could listen. Often the radio occupied a table top and the speaker was housed on the bottom shelf. One unit floor and table models evolved later.

Freed-Eisemann table top radio with an all metal base and a speaker section made of a combination of wood and metal, early 1900's. 21" wide, 11" deep, 20" high.

Walnut and walnut veneered Sparton radio, 1920's. 28" wide, 16" deep, 52" high.

Mahogany veneered Philco radio, 1930's. 26" wide, 13" deep, 41" high.

Walnut and Orientalwood veneered Earl console radio, 1930's. 28" wide, 17" deep, 49" high.

Walnut veneered Motorola table side radio, 1930's. 15" wide, 26" deep, 21" high.

Oak Philco table top radio, 1940's. 20" wide, 12" deep, 12" high.

Radio bench with upholstered seat and brass washed base, 1930's. 24" wide, 12" deep, 19" high.

"Flamewood" veneered mahogany Philco combination radio and record player, 1950's. 36" wide, 16" deep, 35" high.

Radio bench with upholstered seat and metal base, 1920's. 24" wide, 12" deep, 21" high.

RADIO BENCH

This was a low, narrow, backless bench that was used near a radio. It was a handy place to sit while adjusting dials. Most benches from the 1930's and 1940's had upholstered seats, fancy metal bases, often gold trimmed, copper washed or polychromed.

ROCKING CHAIR

A seat that moves backward and forward on two curved runners or rockers is called a rocker or rocking chair. A patented type may sway on a platform in some manner and is referred to as a platform rocker. Some have a patented spring motion instead.

Benjamin Franklin ordered a "crook't foot chair" (crooked) in 1748, so called because the rockers curved. Undoubtedly these runners were attached to common straight chairs at first to convert them into swaying chairs. Early examples were called "carpet cutters" because their thin rockers damaged rugs. At first runners protruded almost equidistant at the front and back, but greater stability was obtained later when the rocker extension was longer in the back.

There are many varieties including the bentwood Thonet rocker, an Austrian development, caned seat and back examples, upholstered varieties, and pressed back types. The latter were popular from the 1890's through the first decade of the 1900's. The circa 1840–1890 Boston rocker had a wooden rolling seat that came up at the back and down in front.

Mahogany stained pressed back rocker with cane seat, early 1900's. 25" arm to arm, 40" high.

Oak rocker with carved grotesque on back splat, early 1900's. 29" arm to arm, 37" high.

Oak rocker with a scooped upholstered seat, early 1900's. 24" arm to arm, 38" high.

Oak pressed back rocker with imitation leather seat, early 1900's. 24" arm to arm, 42" high.

Oak rocker with carved shell in back rail and ball and stick spindles in back and under arms, early 1900's. 26" arm to arm, 45" high.

Oak rocker with upholstered seat, 1920's. 27" arm to arm, 41" high.

Maple folding rocker with slat seat, 1920's. 24" arm to arm, 39" high.

Elm and maple pressed back rocker, early 1900's. 36" high.

Oak S-roll top desk, 1920's. 50" wide, 30" deep, 48" high.

Oak pressed back rocker with cane seat, 1920's. 36" high.

ROLL TOP DESK

Parallel slats glued to a flexible, strong material, such as duck or linen, are a distinguishing characteristic of a roll top desk. The top moves in a groove to open or close. In current terminology, if there is one curve, it is called a C-roll. When there are two curves, an S-roll results. The latter is more sought after and more costly than the former.

Oak S-roll top desk, 1920's. 30" wide, 29" deep, 44" high.

Oak S-roll top desk finished on all sides, early 1900's. 60" wide, 35" deep, 51" high.

ROMAN CHAIR

As pictured and described in the 1908 Sears, Roebuck Catalogue, a Roman chair came with a wide, concave wooden seat and with or without a back. Wood or finish choices were quarter sawed oak, a golden finish, or aniline dyed birch which was called imitation mahogany. Often the back posts and top panels had deep carving and the more expensive chairs came with heavy claw feet.

Mahogany stained birch Roman chair with carved design on back
rail, early 1900's. 24" arm to arm, 36" high.

Oak Roman chair with applied decorations and carved design on
back rail and splat, early 1900's. 24" arm to arm, 35" high.

ROYCROFT

Elbert Hubbard (1856–1915) founded and led the Roycroft Shop from 1895 to 1915. He was an author with a spirited personality who had worked for his brother-in-law, J.D. Larkin, in the Larkin Soap Manufacturing Co. at Buffalo, New York. He helped set up the Larkin Club plan whereby members received premium points they could exchange for Larkin furniture. Hubbard left Larkin in 1892, and in 1895, the year after he visited leaders of England's Arts and Crafts Movement, he established the Roycroft Press. He had been impressed by William Morris' Kelmscott Press, and since Hubbard was an author, he collected a group of artisans together to print handmade books as works of art.

The Roycroft Shop was located at East Aurora, New York. Functional copper household wares, leather goods, and furniture were made there also. The furniture was sold first in 1896, two years before Gustav Stickley fell under the Arts and Crafts influence. Most of the furniture the Roycrofters designed was made of quarter sawed oak, but bird's-eye maple, mahogany and walnut were other woods used. It was fashioned by hand with simplicity of design, high quality workmanship, and durability. With its straight lines and mortise and tenon joints, it resembled Mission, but Hubbard did not use this term until later.

The furniture was marked prominently. The Roycroft Orb and Cross symbol was used on some while others wore a bold "Roycroft" in Gothic script. This was generally placed on the front, rather than in an inconspicuous place in the back or underneath.

The Roycroft artisans outlived their organizer. Elbert Hubbard was aboard the ocean liner *Lusitania* when the Germans sank her in 1915, an atrocity which helped motivate the United States to join the Allies in World War I. Production in the Roycroft Shops decreased in the 1930's until bankruptcy closed them in 1938.

SCREEN

A screen is a covered, portable frame or a series of three or four frames hinged together that allows it to be spread horizontally. It can therefore serve as a moveable partition that conceals, separates, protects, or shelters. For example, a screen might serve as a room divider. In a 1900 catalogue a folding screen of cloth and oak was advertised. It had a "silkaline filling." Another featured a "sateen filling with imported tapestry or figured denim" stretched over the inside frame making a double filling.

Fumed oak three panel screen, 1920's. 60" wide, 68" high.

Three panel screen with painted Oriental designs, 1920's. 51" wide, 70" high.

SERPENTINE FRONT

Currently when the front of a dresser, cabinet, desk or other cabinet piece emulates the curve of a wiggling snake, it is called a serpentine front. Most early catalogue terminology used the phrase "full swell front" to describe a serpentine front, and when only the top two drawers stuck out it was called a "half swell front." This latter is termed a projection front because it projects out over the base. Once in a 1905–1906 catalogue the phrase "serpentine front" was used.

Tiger maple dresser showing serpentine front.

SERVER

A server is a small serving and storage unit in a dining room used with or in place of a buffet.

Bubinga peacock feather and quartered zebrawood veneered server, 1930's. 45" wide, 19" deep, 33" high.

SEWING MACHINE

A sewing machine has a mechanically driven needle used for stitching in order to bind materials together with thread. Thomas Saint, an Englishman, patented the first sewing machine in 1790. Subsequently others experimented and created machines. The first practical example was patented by Elias Howe, an American, in 1846. Other improvements followed. Issac Singer patented the foot-operated treadle in 1851 and also a presser foot to hold fabric in place so that it could be stitched. Sometimes the metal base without the machine section is converted to a bedside or lamp table with a marble or wooden top.

Oak sewing machine case with applied decorations and back rail, early 1900's. 25" wide, 20" deep, 30" high.

Oak sewing machine case with applied beading, 1920's. 23" wide, 18" deep, 30" high.

Mahogany and bleached mahogany sewing machine case, 1930's. 29" wide, 17" deep, 31" high.

SHAVING STAND OR SHELF

Various versions of stands or shelves, ranging in size from floor standing to wall hanging examples, held a man's shaving needs including a lather brush, the soap, a strop and razors.

Oak shaving stand with swing mirror, early 1900's. 65" high.

SIDEBOARD (see Buffet)

A sideboard or buffet is a dining room piece with drawers and cupboards where china, silverware, linens, and other dinner service articles are kept. Among the many authorities who use the two terms interchangably is Joseph Aronson, author of *The Encyclopedia of Furniture.* Most of his examples, however, pre-date the twentieth century and are European in origin.

Research indicates, however, that those pieces called sideboards generally pre-dated 1915 and were ornately carved, had full swell fronts, French beveled plate mirrors and ranged in size from 42" to 60" in width. Their height often reached 85". Those after 1915, called buffets, seem to fit the description in a 1927 catalogue which pictures these storage units as low, narrow pieces with a series of doors and drawers, supported by four to six legs. Some have a narrow mirror on the back and their average height is 41".

Oak sideboard with applied decorations and carving, early 1900's. 56" wide, 26" deep, 82" high. Below: close-up of carved design.

Oak shaving mirror, 1920's. 18" wide, 8" deep, 26" high.

117

Oak sideboard with swell top drawers and applied decorations, early 1900's. 45" wide, 21" deep, 76" high.

Oak sideboard with marble top and incised designs, early 1900's. 48" wide, 19" deep, 80" high.

Oak sideboard with applied decorations, incised designs and paw feet, early 1900's. 54" wide, 27" deep, 67" high.

SMOKER

The smoker or smoking stand became prominent in the 1920's. A metal stand, often including onyx parts, was common. When the smoker became a cabinet stand, an ashtray was usually on top. The cabinet area often included a pipe rack. A humidor resulted when an enclosed copper or copper coated tin-lined section with a moisture pad was added to keep tobacco fresh.

Smokers were made of oak, selected hardwoods or metal. During the late 1920's and 1930's, many exotic veneers were used to decorate these stands. Zebrano or zebrawood was a popular choice. Decals or hand-painted designs were, at times, applied on the panels and legs. Holly, which could be used in its natural light state or dyed in blacks, reds and greens was used for inlay work. Black lacquer, with appropriate scenes, created an Oriental feel, whereas a crackled finish produced a fake look of age.

SPICE CABINET

When spices came in hunks, seed, or leaf form, they were frequently segregated in separate drawers in a small cabinet that could be hung on a wall or stand on a shelf .

118

Oak smoking stand with incised carving, 1920's. 14" wide, 11" deep, 25" high.

Onyx smoking stand, 1940's. 13" square, 28" high.

Walnut stained smoking stand, 1920's. 15" wide, 15" deep, 27" high.

Painted smoking stand, 1930's. 12" wide, 12" deep, 28" high.

Oak spice cabinet, early 1900's. 10" wide, 5" deep, 23" high.

Maple spice cabinet, 1920's. 11" wide, 5" deep, 17" high.

SPINET DESK

A spinet, an ancestor of the piano, was an early stringed instrument with a keyboard. In the early 1800's the cases were frequently converted into shallow desks after the musical sections were removed. In the 1930's spinet desks, or piano desks as they were sometimes called, were manufactured to emulate those "recycled" cases.

Clark's label on spool cabinet.

Mahogany stained maple spinet desk with incised lines, 1920's. 32" wide, 18" deep, 31" high.

SPOOL CABINET

In the late 1800's and early 1900's, country stores had many advertising items, which manufacturers supplied to hold their products. Spool cabinets, provided by companies that produced thread, are an example. These ranged from stands with various numbers of drawers to counter desks with spool ads on them. Some walnut and cherry examples exist. Most, however, were made of oak. An unusual version, patented in 1897 and bearing the name Merrick, was circular or oval. Often these advertising cabinets are used in homes. Small ones become jewelry or scarf boxes while large ones with many drawers serve as tables.

Oak Clark's ONT six-drawer spool cabinet, 1920's. 26" wide, 20" deep, 23" high.

STACK BOOKCASE

These bookcases, advertised in a 1902 catalogue and called extension bookcases, could be purchased in sections including base and top, which did not provide any book storage, and either 9¼", 11¼" or 13¼" high book sections with glass doors that operated on roller bearings. There was a choice of quarter sawed oak or veneered mahogany. It's ironic to note, considering the popularity of oak over mahogany, that the latter cost a nickel more per section.

Oak four section stack bookcase with leaded glass, early 1900's. 25" wide, 13" deep, 35" high.

Oak six section stack bookcase with leaded glass in upper two sections, early 1900's. 34" wide, 12" deep, 57" high.

Oak five section stack bookcase. 34" wide, 12" deep, 47" high.

STICKLEY BROS.

Three of Albert Stickley's brothers — Gustav, Leopold, and J. George — left the furniture company in which all were united, to form companies of their own. Albert headed Stickley Bros., a Grand Rapids, Michigan firm. The factory produced various types of furniture, including late Victorian pieces. Their oak Mission style furniture bore a label that read "Quaint Furniture."

Oak six section stack bookcase with desk in one section, 1920's. 34" wide, 12" deep, 63" high.

Fumed oak bench. Label reads: "Quaint Furniture, Stickley Bros. Co., Grand Rapids, Mich." Early 1900's. 48" arm to arm, 23" deep, 36" high.

STICKLEY, GUSTAV

At one time Gustav Stickley (1858–1942) made ornate walnut furniture as well as other styles. It was not until he visited England in 1898 that he became intrigued with the ideas and works of the Arts and Crafts Movement advocates. Upon his return home, he rebelled against the current American fashions and for two years he experimented with uncluttered, strong, straight utilitarian furniture of oak. He displayed examples of his work at Michigan's Grand Rapids Furniture Exposition in 1900. The name he selected for his products was Craftsman.

Today those who promote and collect his work credit Gustav Stickley with creating a new style of American furniture. When Craftsman sold well, other companies fashioned furniture along the same lines. Soon it became known by the generic title "Mission Furniture."

Gustav Stickley liked a fumed oak finish which was achieved through the use of ammonia vapors. Obvious joinery techniques such as corbels and exposed mortise and tenons were employed. Large metal hinges, drawer pulls, escutcheons, and other hardware, some of which was hand hammered, characterized many of his pieces.

At first, for only a brief time, his works were marketed with a circular Tobey paper label and sold by the Tobey Furniture Co., Chicago. The maker's name was not included. Gustav Stickley then developed a trademark that included a joiner's compass of ancient origin that enclosed the motto "Als ik Kan." Stickley's name was underneath. At times it was branded or burned into the wood. Other times it was applied as a red decal. Its size and design varied slightly through the years. This shop mark was placed in unobtrusive places such as beneath the arms, on the back leg of chairs, on the backs of case pieces, or under table tops. Various Craftsman paper labels appeared and were used separately, but in conjunction with, the trademark. The company, located in Eastwood with a Syracuse, New York postal address, went out of business in 1916.

Gustav Stickley was proud of his structurally strong, straight-lined furniture. He forecast that it would some day receive an "heirloom" rating and would increase in price. He was sure that it would not wear out through use. His prediction has come true, since interest in Mission furniture revived in the late 1960's and early 1970's.

Label found on Gustav Stickley furniture. Inside the joiner's compass are the words "Als ik Kan."

STICKLEY, L & JG

Under the firm name of L. and J.G. Stickley, Leopold and J. George, younger brothers of Gustav Stickley, manufactured quality furniture. They were willing to create lines to accommodate tall and small people. "Handcraft" was this company's name for its Mission style products. These men were capable of designing and creating fine furniture on their own, but their Mission lines frequently included examples that had characteristics similar to those of their sibling's Craftsman products, a fact that irritated their older brother, Gustav. The shop Leopold and J. George owned was in Fayetteville, New York. The company remains in business today. In addition to other styles, a line of Mission that emulates the old is being produced currently.

Oak game table, style 636, marked Gustav Stickley, early 1900's. 48" diameter, 30" high.

Label found on Handcraft table.

Oak table, style 530, marked L. & J.G. Stickley Handcraft, early 1900's. 48" wide, 30" deep, 30" high.

Buffet in the Queen Anne style from 1915–1916 catalogue. (She ruled England from 1702 to 1714.) Black walnut with cabriole legs and moulded drawer fronts. 66" wide, 22" deep, 52" high.

STYLES OF FURNITURE (See Colonial Style)

During the 1910–1930's, furniture manufacturers copied period styles from the seventeenth and eighteenth centuries. In order to acquaint you with the skillful copies of period furniture made in the early 1900's, some illustrations from the 1915–1916 Chittenden & Eastman catalogue are shown. Monarchs' and cabinetmakers' names were used to distinguish these styles.

For information on other styles of furniture, see "Art Deco," "Art Nouveau," and "Waterfall."

Buffet in the Georgian Period style from 1915–1916 catalogue. (George I, II, and III were English rulers between 1714 and 1795.) Black walnut case and burl walnut on front panels. Fluted legs. 60" wide, 22" deep, 52" high.

Buffet in the William and Mary style from 1915–1916 catalogue. (They ruled England from 1689 to 1702.) Quarter sawed oak with graceful underbracing and turned uprights. 66" wide, 24" deep, 53" high.

Right: Buffet in the Adam Period style from 1915–1916 catalogue. (Robert and James Adam were English cabinetmakers in the last half of the eighteenth century.) Solid mahogany with raised beading, rams carvings and spade feet. 62" wide, 21" deep, 46" high.

Buffet in the Louis XVI style from 1915–1916 catalogue. (Louis XVI ruled France from 1774 to 1792.) Genuine mahogany with elaborate detail and rich carving. 66" wide, 26" deep, 49" high.

Bed in the Sheraton Period style from 1915–1916 catalogue. (Thomas Sheraton was an English cabinetmaker from the late 1700's through the first few years of the 1800's.) Circassian walnut with decoration mostly of marquetry and inlay. 52" high.

Right: Oak swivel desk chair with incised designs, early 1900's. 23" arm to arm, 45" high.

SWIVEL DESK CHAIR

A swivel chair turns around horizontally on a pivot in its base and can also tilt back. Some have arms and most roll on casters. They were called spring and screw office chairs in old catalogues.

Oak pressed back swivel desk chair, early 1900's. 24" arm to arm, 45" high.

TABLE (See also Dining Room Table)

Parlor or occasional table is the general name for the many types of tables that serve in the living room. Their titles may come from their shapes, functions, characteristics or styles. Cloverleaf, lamp, tilt top and Duncan Phyfe are consecutive examples of each of these name types.

A "cloverleaf" table resembles the leaf of a clover in configuration. Some of these 1930 tables had tooled leather tops, veneered or solid walnut or mahogany construction. Another descriptive name is "nest of tables," an aid to a hostess when she served coffee in the living room. A stack of three or more tables of gradually diminishing sizes fit one beneath the other into a compact single position or could be separated into individual units. In the 1930's Oriental scenes were frequently painted on tables. When this is done on ceramics, furniture, textiles or other objects, the result is called chinoiserie. A combination of walnut and walnut veneers could be used.

Picture a tier table. It may have two or three circular levels graduating in size from the largest at the base to the smallest at the top. Some are half round to fit against a wall, but this is not common. Furniture companies occasionally called tier tables "dumb waiters," even when their shelves did not revolve, because one could be placed near the hostess' dining room chair so that additional service, dessert or the like was within easy reach. Mahogany, both solid and in veneer form, was a popular wood in the 1920's and 1930's. Striped mahogany veneer was one kind available.

Does a round table with a deep apron that may include drawers remind you of a drum? Drum tables were available in the 1930's and continue in current use. Some had tooled leather tops. Others featured mahogany veneer tops and hardwood bases. It was Thomas Sheraton, an English furniture maker, who introduced the drum table around 1800.

Another shape name was console. It was half round and the flat edge fit against a wall. A mirror often hung above it. Consoles existed in the 1800's and are still made. Hand painted versions were sold in the 1920's and 1930's, some with floral designs on their aprons and legs.

End tables that stood beside davenports and chairs often had one flat side also. It was a handy place on which to put a lamp and reading materials. A matching pair often flanked a sofa.

Usage is another clue as to how tables received their names. The low coffee or cocktail table, about 17" to 21" high, was a 1930's innovation that is still currently popular. In 1920, the Eighteenth Amendment to the United States Constitution outlawed the manufacture, transportation and selling of alcoholic beverages. When this law was repealed in 1933, the cocktail table soon invaded some homes. For those who did not imbibe, a coffee table was available instead. Because of their height, their tops were easy to see and they tended to be decorative. Hand tooled genuine leather tops often featured a gold colored outline.

A less expensive synthetic leather was available also. Exotic veneer work formed tops, too. Inlay — patterns set flush into the surface of the surrounding wood — was attractive. Walnut or walnut stained tables sometimes had white painted bases. Tops with relief carving, molded or carved sculpture raised above its background, featured people, patriotic emblems, scenes, flowers or fruits. A glass cover kept the flat top available for use. Sometime this latter was a removable tray that could be used to serve guests.

A sofa table was found in many 1920's homes. It was positioned behind the sofa and it often held a lamp, clock and some decorative mementos. Today, it can be cut down to the size of a coffee table. Then again without alteration it may serve as a table for plants and flowers or for any other purpose the owner desires.

A lamp table, a fern or plant stand, a table with a V-shaped trough to hold books, and game tables that might fold up in some manner when not in use were all useful tables with a particular purpose.

Of course, Mission tables of the early 1900's, which were most often made of oak, had heavy, straight and practical lines. Since oak was a popular wood as the 1800's terminated, many parlor tables were made of that wood or its look-a-likes, ash and elm. Some too were artificially grained to imitate oak.

Oak cloverleaf table, early 1900's. 22" wide, 31" high.

Maple cloverleaf table with metal trim on edges and ball and claw feet, 1920's. 28" wide, 30" high.

Mahogany tier table with tripod base, 1940's. 20" diameter bottom shelf, 12" diameter top shelf, 42" high.

Mahogany nest of tables with leather tops and drawer in smallest table, 1940's. 27" wide, 15" deep, 24" high.

Walnut end or half table with carved bird on front leg, 1940's. 26" wide, 13" deep, 25" high.

Mahogany drum table with top that rotates, 1940's. 30" diameter, 28" high.

Mahogany oval end table with mirror top. Dated under top: June 11, 1940. 20" wide, 16" deep, 23" high.

Walnut end table with four piece matched burl walnut veneered top, holly line design and inlaid flowers, 1930's. 33" wide, 22" deep, 29" high.

Cherry occasional table made by Willett, 1950's. One of a pair. 20" wide, 23" deep, 27" high.

Striped mahogany and V-matched zebrano veneered occasional table with brass rail, 1930's. One of a pair. 20" wide, 15" deep, 30" high.

Mahogany occasional table with serpentine front and decorated leather top, 1940's. One of a pair. 16" wide, 22" deep, 25" high.

Mahogany coffee table with decorated leather top made by Heritage, late 1940's. 30" diameter, 17" high.

Mahogany coffee table with two fretwork lift out trays and cabriole legs, 1920's. 37" wide, 19" deep, 17" high.

Mahogany occasional table with four piece matched mahogany veneered top and inlaid holly banding, 1940's. One of a pair. 18" diameter, 28" high.

Walnut veneered coffee table with cream base and cabriole legs, 1930's. 39" wide, 18" deep, 18" high.

Walnut coffee table with carved man's head, 1940's. 25" wide, 15" deep, 19" high.

Walnut coffee table with four piece matched burl top, inlaid designs and fretwork, and carved designs on apron and legs, 1930's. 35" wide, 20" deep, 17" high.

Mahogany Queen Anne style drop leaf coffee table with cabriole legs, 1930's. 48" wide, 16" deep, 18" high, 10" drop leaves.

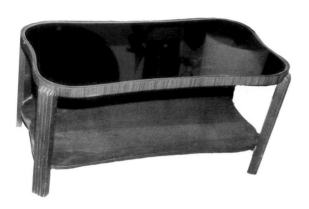

Mahogany stained coffee table with blue glass top, 1950's. 32" wide, 17" deep, 17" high.

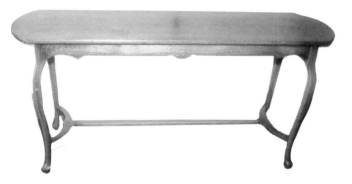

Oak sofa table, 1920's. 60" wide, 18" deep, 29" high.

Oak parlor table, early 1900's. 16" square, 30" high.

Oak parlor table with designs on legs and apron, early 1900's. 23" square, 29" high.

Oak parlor table with incised lines and carving on base, late 1800's or early 1900's. 16" square, 29" high.

Oak parlor table with stick and ball decorations and twisted legs, early 1900's. 24" square, 29" high.

Oak parlor table with carved eagle support legs, early 1900's. 20" diameter, 28" high.

Oak center table, early 1900's. 45" wide, 28" deep, 30" high.

Oak parlor table with incised designs on apron and ball and claw feet, 1920's. 36" wide, 24" deep, 30" high.

Oak corner table with base shelf, early 1900's. 44" wide, 31" deep, 31" high.

TEA CART (see Hostess Wagon)

This was a small serving push cart on wheels that had shelves used for dishes, beverages or food. Sometimes it included a removable tray. Hostess cart was another name given to it.

Maple tea cart with new casters and a retractable handle, 1940's. 33" wide, 19" deep, 29" high, 10" drop leaves.

TELEPHONE

A telephone is an instrument that conveys voices over distances by converting sound into electrical impulses. A transmitter and receiver are necessary. Only a year after its invention, Alexander Graham Bell amazed visitors at America's 1876 Centennial Exposition in Philadelphia by demonstrating his invention. Later, long wooden cases held the working parts of wall telephones. In rural areas many of these were still in use in the late 1940's or early 1950's. Now they are collectible. Most have oak cases but occasionally a walnut one is found. Other passe telephones are collectible also, especially a desk type now popularly called a candlestick phone, with its thin candle-like stem, which was often black.

TELEPHONE SET

A telephone set, made up of a small table and accompanying chair or stool, was designed to accommodate the telephone, the book and the talker. Many one-piece sets with a chair and a table united are also available. Plain examples were of selected hardwood, some were painted and others were lacquered and had Oriental designs.

Oak wall telephone made by Western Electric Company, 1920's. 9" wide, 5" deep, 19" high.

Walnut veneer and walnut stained maple telephone stand, 1940's. 27" wide, 18" deep, 31" high.

Oak telephone stand, 1920's. Stand — 18" wide, 15" deep, 30" high. Stool — 14" square, 18" high.

THONET BENTWOOD FURNITURE

Around 1840, Michael Thonet of Vienna, Austria, steam bent wooden rods to form chairs, tables, and other furniture that was scientifically designed to use the strength of the individual parts. Many pieces of early mass produced furniture resulted. Bentwood furniture is still produced today.

Fir tramp art cabinet in two sections, late 1920's or early 1930's. 32" wide, 16" deep, 72" high.

Thonet bentwood chair with cane back and seat, early 1900's. One of a set of four. 36" high.

TRAMP ART

Chip carving and layering of thin pieces of wood are two main characteristics of tramp art. Examples were often made from the wood of throw- or give-away cigar boxes. At times soft wood vegetable or orange crates were used. Completed pieces were usually stained dark. Some tramp art dated back to the 1860's and continued into the 1930's. Any available tool that could be used to make a notch was employed, but just a pocket knife was sufficient. Many examples of this folk art were made by itinerants such as migrating workers, traveling salesmen, or gypsies as well as prisoners of war, farmers, or their hired hands. Applied decorations or inlaid shells, metal or bits of contrasting wood were present occasionally. Frames, boxes, and small chests, cupboards, tables and dressers have been found. An unusually tall tramp art cabinet, illustrated here, with two almost out-of-reach parallel drawers at the top, was on display in a shop in Alaska.

Tramp art child's dresser, dated Feb. 14, 1925 on back. 21" wide, 10" deep, 46" high.

UMBRELLA STAND

An umbrella stand held closed umbrellas. If they were wet, a metal drip pan at the base caught the dripping water.

Oak folding umbrella stand with replaced drip pan, early 1900's. 18" wide, 9" deep, 32" high.

UPHOLSTERED FURNITURE

Well-padded furniture, sometimes called "overstuffed," was featured in mail order catalogues of the late 1800's and early 1900's. Complete parlor suites were available with a choice of such pieces as arm chair, davenport, rocker, lounge chair or button back chair. They featured thick felted cotton padding, removable spring cushions and a choice of covering like colored velour, Persian tapestry, two-toned veronas, plain or crushed mohair, crushed mohair plush, silk damask, silk brocatelles, a substitute leather called chase leather, or geniune leather.

A sample of upholstered furniture pictured in a 1929 Ward's catalogue.

V

VANITY TABLE (see Dressing Table)

A table with a mirror or mirrors was referred to as a vanity table. Usually it contained small drawers for cosmetics, hair brushes, combs and other personal articles. Some had drop centers with small drawers at each side of the top surface.

VENEERS

Veneer is a thin layer of wood cut from logs. In the early 1900's, fragile, rare, beautiful woods, generally sliced in sheets one twenty-eighth of an inch thick, were glued over less attractive, cheaper furniture boards. This added strength to fragile woods and extended their use as well.

As the 1920's neared their end, the use of domestic and imported veneers had reached a point where most American produced furniture was partially or totally veneered. This trend continued through the 1930's, the decade in which more than 25 different veneers from the Indies, France, England, Africa, Central and South America, India, Ceylon, Puerto Rico, Honduras, Borneo, Australia, Tasmania, Mexico, Hawaii, the Philippines, Burma, and Canada were used in the furniture industry.

The multitude of patterns utilized included burl, quarter sawed, crotch, curly, figured, diamond-matched, fiddleback, quilted, mottled, V-matched, four way butt, basketweave, swirl and many varieties of matched designs. The 1940's saw the demise of the excessive use of veneers, and in that decade only about ten veneers were in general use.

Mahogany vanity with swing mirror and cabriole legs, 1920's. 33" wide, 19" deep, 55" high.

W

WALL HANGINGS

This is a broad category that includes pictures, mirrors and other ornamental or utilitarian items that hang on the wall.

Fumed oak frame featuring three horse scenes, 1920's. 38" wide, 15" high.

Oak and gilt painted multilinear frame, early 1900's. 31" wide, 27" high.

Oak and gilt painted multilinear frame, early 1900's. 26" wide, 30" high.

Oak frame with applied decorations and beveled mirror, early 1900's. 33" wide, 31" high.

Wall pocket painted black with gold accents, early 1900's. Picture of sheep is entitled "A May Day," dated 1908 by A. Fox, Philadelphia. 17" wide, 15" high, pulls out to 10" at top.

WARDROBE

A wardrobe was a storage cupboard where clothes hung in the days before closets were common in homes. It often included several drawers and a door mirror. Most of the early century wardrobes were constructed of oak or ash.

Some were too large to carry up a flight of stairs or around corners. This problem was solved by the knock-down varieties, referred to as portable wardrobes in some catalogues. The letters *KD* were a shipping term for "knock down." Currently, the terms *collapsible* or *breakdown* describe this feature.

Oak one-door wardrobe, 1920's. 36" wide, 17" deep, 77" high.

Oak breakdown two-door wardrobe with pilasters, applied decorations and paw feet, early 1900's. 45" wide, 19" deep, 107" high.

Oak breakdown two-door wardrobe with applied decorations, early 1900's. 48" wide, 18" deep, 85" high.

WASHSTAND COMMODE (see Commode)

A stand, ordinarily with a towel bar at the back and a combination of drawers and doors, held a bowl and pitcher in the days before water was piped into houses. When a mirror was a part of the towel bar back, these stands were called hotel or toilet washstands. Stands were available in bird's-eye maple, mahogany, oak and northern hardwood with a golden oak finish.

Right: Oak washstand with projection, serpentine drawer front and attached towel rack, early 1900's. 32" wide, 18" deep, 60" high.

WATERFALL STYLE FURNITURE

"Waterfall" describes a rounded edge used on furniture tops, a style available from the 1930's through the 1950's. The curve had a surface of various European and Eastern veneers. These veneers were also used to decorate the drawer and door panels of case pieces such as dressers, chests of drawers and head and footboards of beds. Cedar chests featured waterfall tops also. In reviewing furniture catalogues, the first mention and example of waterfall, as a style of furniture, was found in a 1938 book. The last picture of a waterfall bedroom set was seen in a 1959 catalogue where only one set was available.

Dozens of veneers with varying patterns were used during this period. Among the most popular were V-matched Oriental walnut, plain cut walnut, butt walnut, V-matched zebrawood or zebrano, satinwood, V-matched paldao, diamond matched sliced red gum, curly maple, bird's-eye maple, plain cut mahogany and sliced avodire.

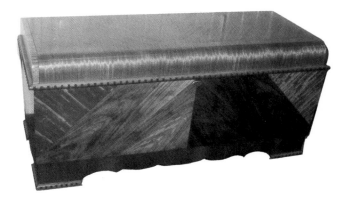

Waterfall style cedar chest with Oriental walnut veneered surfaces, 1940's. 47" wide, 19" deep, 22" high.

WHATNOT

A whatnot for the display of curios was not as prevalent during the twentieth century as it was in the nineteenth. Those that were found in the early 1900's were called parlor cabinets. They stood on legs and were constructed of birch with an imitation mahogany finish. The least expensive had one mirror but the costlier whatnots had a French beveled plate mirror behind each shelf.

WICKER

Wicker is a generic name, not a raw material. Strong, flexible twigs, called osiers, come from some willow trees such as Lemley, purple, and green varieties. It is soft, tough, and accepts stain well. Another material for wicker is rattan, a very strong vine-like palm that grows tall and thin and bends well without breaking.

Cane and reed come from rattan. Cane comes in different sizes of thin strips split from the outer bark of rattan. It is glossy on the top and fibrous on the bottom and can be woven to form seat bottoms and backs, or it can be wrapped around wooden parts such as legs or stretchers. Reed is very pliant and may be round, flat, or oval. It is the inner part or pith of rattan and can be painted or stained.

Rush is a perennial plant that usually grows in wet areas. It is used to weave chair seats. Today some of the rush is man-made of spiral paper.

Fiber, art fiber, and fiber reed are names for reed made by machine from twisted, treated paper. Some have a flexible wire added for support. In 1917 Marshall B. Lloyd invented a loom to weave the less costly and more pliable man-made fiber into material that could be applied to furniture frames. With the invention of this machine, the hand work of making wicker furniture was no longer necessary because the machine could do the work thirty times faster than a man could by hand. Because of this, Lloyd's loom dominated the industry by the late 1920's.

Mahogany stained (aniline dyed) birch whatnot or parlor cabinet, early 1900's. 26" wide, 11" deep, 50" high.

These standardized pieces were neither as attractive nor as ornate as the hand-crafted examples from the last part of the 1800's and the early 1900's. That is one reason why wicker work decreased in popularity after the 1920's. Its popularity has been recently revived, and today's collectors seek out the more ornate, hand-woven examples with their fancy, delicate patterns.

Heywood-Wakefield wicker desk and chair with the original brown material made on the Lloyd loom, 1920's. Desk — 33" wide, 22" deep, 35" high. Chair — 36" high.

Three-piece Heywood-Wakefield wicker sofa, arm chair and rocker with the original natural brown material made on the Lloyd loom, 1920's. Sofa — 81" arm to arm, 37" high. Arm chair — 31" wide, 38" high. Rocker — 29" wide, 35" high.

BIBLIOGRAPHY

BOOKS

Aronson, Joseph.
   The Encyclopedia of Furniture. Third Edition.
   New York: Crown Publishers, Inc., 1965.

Cathers, David M.
   Furniture of the American Arts and Crafts Movement
   Stickley and Roycroft Mission Oak.
   New York: New American Library, 1981.

Fendelman, Helaine W.
   Tramp Art An Itinerant's Folk Art.
   New York: E.P. Dutton & Co., Inc., 1975.

Limbert, Charles P.
   Limberts Holland Dutch Arts and Crafts Furniture;
   Booklet 112.
   New York: Turn of the Century Editions, 1981.

Shull, Thelma.
   Victorian Antiques.
   Rutland, VT: Charles E. Tuttle Company, 1963.

Swedberg, Robert W. and Harriett Swedberg.
   American Oak Furniture Styles and Prices Revised Edition.
   Radnor, PA: Wallace-Homestead Book Co., 1991.

———
   American Oak Furniture Styles and Prices, Book II,
   Revised Edition
   Radnor, PA: Wallace-Homestead Book Co., 1991.

———
   American Oak Furniture Styles and Prices, Book III,
   Revised Edition.
   Radnor, PA: Wallace-Homestead Book Co., 1991.

———
   Furniture of the Depression Era -
   Furniture and Accessories of the 1920's, 1930's & 1940's.
   Paducah, KY: Collector Books, 1987.

———
   Wicker Furniture Styles and Prices, Revised Edition.
   Radnor, PA: Wallace-Homestead Book Co., 1987.

REFERENCE WORKS

Guralnik, David B., ed.
   Webster's New World Dictionary of the American
   Language, Second College Edition.
   New York, NY: Simon and Schuster, 1980.

   The World Book Encyclopedia.
   Chicago: Field Enterprises Educational Corporation,
   1965.

CATALOGUES

Amory, Cleveland, ed.
   1902 Sears, Roebuck Catalogue.
   New York: Crown Publishers, Inc.

Chittenden & Eastman Company Furniture Distributors.
   Catalogues.
   Burlington, Iowa: 1892 through 1958.

Israel, Fred L., ed.
   1897 Sears, Roebuck Catalogue.
   New York: Chelsea House Publishers, 1976.

Montgomery Ward & Co.,
   Catalogue Number 99.
   Chicago: Fall and Winter, 1923-1924.

Montgomery Ward & Co.,
   Catalogue Number 110.
   Chicago: Spring and Summer, 1929.

Montgomery Ward & Co.,
   Catalog Number 118.
   Chicago: Spring and Summer, 1933.

Schroeder, Joseph J., Jr., ed.
   1908 Sears, Roebuck Catalogue.
   Chicago: The Gun Digest Company, 1969.

Sears, Roebuck and Company.
   Catalogue No. 154.
   Chicago: Spring and Summer, 1927.

VALUE GUIDE

Oak chiffonier w/projection front top drawer $650.00
Mahogany veneered chifforette w/3 drawers $195.00
Child's oak rocker w/grotesque face $225.00
Elm and maple pressed back, cane seat youth rocker $325.00

5-pc. sectional oak file cabinet $695.00
Mahogany framed fireplace screen w/oil painting $490.00
Oak framed fireplace screen w/tapestry covering $265.00
Oak game table w/scooped out troughs for poker chips $495.00
Mahogany veneered, mahogany stained hardwoods game table $125.00

PAGE 78–79
Tiger maple Governor Winthrop fall front secretary $695.00
Oak hall mirror w/applied decorations, 31" x 25" $325.00
Oak hall mirror w/applied decorations, 24" x 38" $350.00
Oak hall mirror w/applied decorations, 32" x 22" $325.00
Oak rectangular hall mirror $175.00
Oak hall tree, Tomlin Cabinet Making Company $2,100.00
Oak 2-part "hall tree" $1,195.00

PAGE 80–81
Oak hall tree w/lift lid bench, incised lines, applied decorations $1,190.00
Oak hall tree w/lift lid bench, applied decorations $2,495.00
Oak hall tree w/lift lid bench, applied decorations, paw feet ...$1,250.00
Oak hall tree w/lift lid bench, applied decorations $1,750.00
Oak hall tree w/applied decorations, metal umbrella holders ...$525.00
Oak corner hall tree w/lift lid bench, applied decorations $1,295.00
Oak hall tree w/applied decorations, arms hold umbrellas $585.00
Hard rock maple nest of tables $350.00
Hard rock maple lamp table $95.00

PAGE 82–83
Hard rock maple end table $95.00
Hard rock maple corner table $125.00
Hard rock maple china cabinet $750.00
Hard rock maple knee hole desk $350.00
Hard rock maple high chair $165.00
Oak chiffonier $385.00
Oak chiffonier w/serpentine front, applied decorations $595.00
Walnut veneered highboy w/shell on knees of cabriole legs ..$1,475.00

PAGE 84–85
Oak Mission style high chair $250.00
Oak pressed back high chair $240.00
Oak high chair, go cart combination $475.00
Hard rock high chair, go cart combination $135.00
Oak Seller's kitchen cabinet $895.00
Oak "Hoosier type" kitchen cabinet w/wooden working surface $650.00

PAGE 86–87
Oak Seller's kitchen cabinet w/porcelain working surface $495.00
Oak "Hoosier type" kitchen cabinet w/porcelain working surface $725.00
Limed oak Napanee kitchen cabinet $355.00
Mahogany hostess wagon w/pull out handles $400.00
Oak hostess wagon w/incised lines, applied decorations $300.00
Oriental designed hostess wagon w/removable tray $440.00
Walnut, maple tea cart w/removable glass tray $265.00
Oak hotel washstand $650.00

PAGE 88–89
Oak three door ice box $395.00
Ash single door ice box $695.00
Oak ice chest $345.00
Five pc. ice cream set w/oak top table $450.00
Larkin fall front oak desk, bookcase base $690.00

PAGE 90–91
Oak library table w/1 drawer $850.00
Oak library table w/1 drawer, pillars and scroll feet $550.00
Oak Mission style library table $135.00
Oak library table w/cabriole legs, paw feet, 29" high $475.00
Oak library table w/incised designs $345.00
Oak library table w/bulbous legs $475.00
Oak library table w/cabriole legs, paw feet, 30" high $525.00
Limbert fumed oak desk $1,190.00

PAGE 92–93
2-pc. mahogany parlor set w/holly inlaid designs $350.00

2-pc. upholstered living room set w/grotesques $1,850.00
3-pc. upholstered living room set w/carved designs $3,500.00
3-pc. oak parlor set w/black leather seats, tufted backs $1,600.00

PAGE 94–95
Metal magazine rack w/floral design $18.00
Cedar combination magazine rack and sewing stand $90.00
Birch margazine rack w/caned sides $45.00
Walnut Martha Washington sewing cabinet $195.00
Oak double door medicine cabinet $225.00
Kitchen table w/porcelain top and tubular metal legs $295.00
Metal artificially grained bed w/floral designs $75.00
Metal bed colored green w/gilt accents ....NP

PAGE 96–97
Metal washstand w/enamel bowl and pitcher $110.00
Oak Mission fall front desk $590.00
Oak Morris type reclining chair $275.00
Oak Murphy type bed with serpentine front $1,295.00
Oak music stand $400.00
Oak music cabinet $290.00

PAGE 98–99
Walnut veneered night stand w/paper banding (1 of pair), pair $975.00
Oak marble top night stand $225.00
Oak 3-pc. upholstered parlor set $595.00
Oak pedestal $650.00
Oak pedestal w/twisted pillar $450.00
Quarter sawed oak pedestal w/grotesque head $150.00
Quarter sawed oak triple pillar pedestal w/claw feet $450.00

PAGE 100–101
Edison oak phonograph $1,050.00
Victor oak table model phonograph $275.00
Brunswick oak phonograph $325.00
Mahogany Victrola phonograph $265.00
Oak photographer's chair w/twisted legs $250.00
Oak photographer's chair $185.00
Duncan Phyfe style side chair (from set of 4), set $595.00
Duncan Phyfe style side chair, lyre back, (from set of 4), set $225.00

PAGE 102–103
Duncan Phyfe drop leaf table $275.00
Oak piano stool w/ball and claw feet $135.00
Maple piano stool w/back $275.00
Oak lift lid piano bench w/cabriole legs $225.00
Oak pier mirror w/marble shelf $1,850.00
Oak and elm pie safe w/round screened ventilation sections $395.00
Oak planter $850.00

PAGE 104–105
Oak plate rail w/mirror $225.00
Oak plate rail w/leaded glass doors $950.00
Oak platform rocker $375.00
Oak pressed back platform rocker, 26" arm to arm, 48" high $195.00
Oak pressed back platform rocker, 25" arm to arm, 43" high $500.00
Oak coin operated player piano $12,500.00
Polychrome frame $60.00

PAGE 106–107
Maple double pressed back rocker w/Man of the Wind $475.00
Oak pressed back office chair w/mermaids $650.00
Bird's-eye maple rocker w/pressed cane seat $135.00
Oak princess dresser w/serpentine front, applied decorations ...$375.00
Oak princess dresser w/bow front, swing mirror $350.00
Oak princess dresser w/serpentine front, decks, swing mirror ..$990.00

PAGE 108–109
Walnut Priscilla sewing stand $55.00
Mahogany Priscilla sewing stand $50.00
Freed-Eisemann table top radio $175.00
Walnut, walnut veneered Sparton radio $695.00

Walnut, Orientalwood veneered Earl console radio $395.00
Mahogany veneered Philco radio $295.00
Walnut veneered Motorola table side radio $225.00

PAGE 110–111
Oak Philco table top radio $125.00
"Flamewood" Philco combination radio/record player $425.00
Radio bench w/upholstered seat, metal base $125.00
Radio bench w/upholstered seat, brass washed base $75.00
Oak rocker w/carved grotesque on back splat $485.00
Oak rocker w/scooped upholstered seat $165.00
Mahogany stained pressed back rocker w/cane seat $325.00
Oak pressed back rocker w/imitation leather seat $105.00

PAGE 112–113
Oak rocker w/carved shell in back rail $295.00
Maple folding rocker $110.00
Oak rocker w/upholstered seat $225.00
Elm and maple pressed back rocker $125.00
Oak pressed back rocker w/cane seat $65.00
Oak S-roll top desk, finished sides $4,500.00
Oak S-roll top desk, 50" wide, 30" deep, 48" high $1,500.00
Oak S-roll top desk, 30" wide, 29" deep, 44" high $1,300.00

PAGE 114–115
Mahogany stained birch Roman chair $110.00
Oak Roman chair w/applied decorations $650.00
Three panel screen w/painted Oriental design $125.00
Fumed oak three panel screen $495.00
Tiger maple dresser .... NP

PAGE 116–117
Bubinga peacock feather and quartered zebrawood server $225.00
Mahogany and bleached mahogany sewing machine case $195.00
Oak sewing machine case w/applied decorations $350.00
Oak sewing machine case w/applied beading $200.00
Oak shaving stand w/swing mirror $300.00
Oak shaving mirror $250.00
Oak sideboard w/applied decorations, carving $1,975.00

PAGE 118–119
Oak sideboard w/swell top drawers, applied decorations $1,250.00
Oak sideboard w/applied decoration, incised designs, paw feet $1,095.00
Oak sideboard w/marble top, incised designs $1,800.00
Onyx smoking stand $135.00
Painted smoking stand $58.00
Walnut stained smoking stand $125.00
Oak smoking stand w/incised carving $245.00
Oak spice cabinet $295.00
Maple spice cabinet $225.00

PAGE 120–121
Mahogany stained maple spinet desk $280.00
Oak Clark's ONT 6-drawer spool cabinet $1,395.00
Oak 4-section stack bookcase w/leaded glass $350.00
Oak 6-section stack bookcase w/leaded glass $750.00
Oak 6-section stack bookcase w/desk $895.00
Oak 5-section stack bookcase $795.00
Fumed oak bench, Stickley Bros. Quaint Furniture $995.00

PAGE 122–123
Oak game table, Gustav Stickley $1,200.00
Oak table, L. & J.G. Stickley Handcraft $475.00
Buffet, William & Mary style .... NP
Buffet, Queen Anne style .... NP
Buffet, Georgian Period style .... NP
Buffet, Adam Period style .... NP

PAGE 124–125
Buffet, Louis XVI style .... NP
Bed, Sheraton Period style .... NP
Oak pressed back swivel desk chair $175.00

Oak swivel desk chair w/incised designs $295.00
Oak cloverleaf table $135.00

PAGE 126–127
Maple clover leaf table w/metal trim, ball and claw feet $80.00
Mahogany nest of tables w/leather tops $285.00
Mahogany drum table w/top that rotates $150.00
Mahogany tier table w/tripod base $68.00
Walnut end or half table $275.00
Mahogany oval end table w/mirror top $145.00
Walnut end table w/4-pc. matched burl walnut veneered top $350.00
Mahogany, V-matched zebrano occasional table (1 of pair), pair ...$1,275.00
Mahogany coffee table w/decorated leather top $140.00
Cherry occasional table (1 of pair), pair $695.00
Mahogany occasional table w/serpentine front (1 of pair), pair ..$195.00

PAGE 128–129
Mahogany occasional table (1 of pair), pair $125.00
Walnut coffee table w/carved man's head $140.00
Mahogany Queen Anne style drop leaf coffee table $175.00
Mahogany coffee table w/2 fretwork lift out trays $400.00
Walnut veneered coffee table w/cream base $150.00
Walnut coffee table w/4-pc. match burl top $250.00
Mahogany stained coffee table w/blue glass top $325.00
Oak sofa table $500.00
Oak parlor table $145.00
Oak parlor table w/designs on legs and apron $125.00
Oak parlor table w/incised lines, carving on base $165.00
Oak parlor table w/stick and ball decorations, twisted legs $375.00

PAGE 130–131
Oak parlor table w/carved eagle support legs $245.00
Oak parlor table w/incised designs on apron, ball and claw feet $650.00
Oak center table $750.00
Oak corner table w/base shelf $450.00
Maple tea cart, retractable handle $175.00
Oak wall telephone, Western Electric Company $285.00
Walnut veneer, walnut stained maple telephone stand $175.00
Oak telephone stand $165.00

PAGE 132–133
Thonet bentwood chair w/cane back, seat (from set of 4), set $495.00
Fir tramp art cabinet $795.00
Tramp art child's dresser $1,300.00
Oak folding umbrella stand, replaced drip pan $127.00
Sample of upholstered furniture .... NP

PAGE 134–135
Mahogany vanity w/swing mirror, cabriole legs $795.00
Fumed oak frame, three horses scene $175.00
Oak and gilt painted multilinear frame, 31" wide, 27" high $125.00
Oak and gilt painted multilinear frame, 26" wide, 30" high $125.00
Oak frame w/applied decorations, beveled mirror $175.00
Wall pocket painted black w/gold accents $110.00
Oak breakdown two-door wardrobe w/pilasters $1,495.00

PAGE 136–137
Oak one-door wardrobe $839.00
Oak breakdown two-door wardrobe w/applied decorations ...$1,595.00
Oak washstand w/projection, serpentine drawer front, towel rack ...$325.00
Waterfall style cedar chest $235.00
Mahogany stained birch (aniline dyed) whatnot or parlor cabinet $385.00

PAGE 138
3-pc. Heywood-Wakefield wicker set $1,250.00
Heywood-Wakefield wicker desk and chair $350.00

Schroeder's Antiques Price Guide

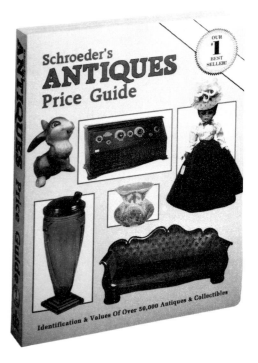

Schroeder's Antiques Price Guide has become THE household name in the antiques & collectibles field. Our team of editors work year-round with more than 200 contributors to bring you our #1 best-selling book on antiques & collectibles.

With more than 50,000 items identified & priced, Schroeder's is a must for the collector & dealer alike. If it merits the interest of today's collector, you'll find it in Schroeder's. Each subject is represented with histories and background information. In addition, hundreds of sharp original photos are used each year to illustrate not only the rare and unusual, but the everyday "fun-type" collectibles as well -- not postage stamp pictures, but large close-up shots that show important details clearly.

Our editors compile a new book each year. Never do we merely change prices. Accuracy is our primary aim. Prices are gathered over the entire year previous to publication, from ads and personal contacts. Then each category is thoroughly checked to spot inconsistencies, listings that may not be entirely reflective of actual market dealings, and lines too vague to be of merit. Only the best of the lot remains for publication. You'll find Schroeder's Antiques Price Guide the one to buy for factual information and quality.

No dealer, collector or investor can afford not to own this book. It is available from your favorite bookseller or antiques dealer at the low price of $12.95. If you are unable to find this price guide in your area, it's available from Collector Books, P.O. Box 3009, Paducah, KY 42002-3009 at $12.95 plus $2.00 for postage and handling.

8½ x 11", 608 Pages   **$12.95**

COLLECTOR BOOKS
A Division of Schroeder Publishing Co., Inc.